GEORGIAN IMPRINTS

Printing and Publishing at Bath, 1729-1815

The frontispiece above is taken from *Connubia florum latino carmine demonstrate*, a book of Latin verse by Demetrius de la Croix on the sexual reproduction of plants. Edited by Sir Richard Clayton and printed at Bath by Samuel Hazard in 1791, it called forth this odd image by the Bath engraver William Hibbert purporting to show Barometz or Scythian Lamb, a life form once thought to be part plant and part animal, but in reality an Asian fern.

The title-page vignette originally appeared in *Rebellion in Bath, or The Battle of the Upper-Rooms*, a satirical poem published pseudonymously in 1808 by Richard Warner, curate of St James's church.

GEORGIAN IMPRINTS

Printing and Publishing at Bath, 1729-1815

by Trevor Fawcett

Wee thre Bath Deities bee:
Humbug; Follee, & Vanitee. *Old Song*

RUTON: 2008

For Mary

A sweet medium paper, a book of fine size,
And a print that I thought would have suited her eyes

(Christopher Anstey, *The New Bath Guide*, epilogue to 2nd edition)

First published in the United Kingdom in 2008 by RUTON,
25 Northampton Street, Bath, BA1 2SW, and printed by
Ralph Allen Press Ltd., 1 Locksbrook Court, Bath, BA1 3EN.

ISBN 0-9526326-4-0

CONTENTS

INTRODUCTION

Around 1700 – no longer confined by the Licensing Act to London, Oxbridge and York – printing presses gradually began to appear in other cities and towns across the country. A century later they were commonplace throughout the provinces, integral to most aspects of social life and vital to local economies. Compared with some of its West Country neighbours Bath made a slow typographical start, but by the 1740s it was catching up and by the 1770s had become a significant contributor to the national output of print at almost all levels, from humdrum but profitable jobbing work to the production of fine books and widely read newspapers. Long known for bookshops and circulating libraries, the spa built a reputation for skilled, reliable printing that attracted London interest and brought commissions that would never have been undertaken otherwise.

Any estimate of the volume of printed matter issuing from Bath's presses year by year would only mislead. Surviving examples of printed ephemera (theatre posters apart) give little idea of the large demand for simple commercial printing that occupied and sustained most printing offices. As for other work, the total of c.1200 books and pamphlets identified for this study must be far from complete, and is in any case a statistic of questionable value, since it lumps together publications of very unequal size and format, from flimsy penny booklets to solid works in several volumes, and makes no allowance for the number of copies printed or for subsequent reprints, new editions, and continuations. Even the effort that went into producing the standard four-page newspapers is hard to estimate as their sheet size and text capacity steadily increased and because their circulations can only be guessed.

Although engravers come into the story as important suppliers of illustrations for books, this account focuses mainly on the business careers of the letterpress printers, including such notable exponents of the craft as Boddely, Hazard and the two Cruttwells. Some of their output was predictable enough – handbills and public notices, moral tales, criminal trials, sermons by local clergy, schoolbooks, treatises on the spa waters, visitors' guidebooks, directories of residents, slim volumes of verse, short-lived magazines, and of course newspapers – starting with Boddely's Bath Journal *in 1744 and rising, with various defunct titles on the way, to the four different Bath papers available from 1812 onwards. On the other hand many less obvious subjects turn up in the roster of Bath imprints as time went on, often resulting from collaborations with London's publishing booksellers. Examples might include a* Koran *in English, a comprehensive Hebrew dictionary, an account of Chinese customs, a bowdlerised Shakespeare, a novel by Pestalozzi, botanical handbooks on British mints and seaweeds, and two pioneering volumes illustrated by lithography.*

Whether a resident author was printed in Bath or not depended on such considerations as the expected readership, prospects of national sales, the convenience of overseeing publication on the spot, local printing expertise (e.g. in handling foreign alphabets, mathematical symbols, music, etc.), existing connections with the book trade beyond Bath, and, crucially, the financial commitment involved. Bath printers published only a minority of books entirely at their own risk and even then partly as self-advertisement (as in the case of guidebooks and directories), though it is true that Cruttwell, for example, subsidised Richard Warner's History of Bath *(1801) and spent out on expensive new type for a prestige work like the Bishop Wilson* Bible *(1781-2) – notwithstanding a contemporary view that it was 'not the Age for Booksellers to make Fortunes by the Sale of Bibles, Prayer Books, &c.'. The* Bible *was financed, at least in part, by advance subscription, a safeguard adopted in such other ventures as Sarah*

Fielding's Xenophon *(1762) and Collinson's* Somerset *(1792) and necessarily resorted to in newspaper publishing. The printer's risk was further reduced when an author or London publisher underwrote the expense of printing and promotion, and perhaps even supplied the paper, always a costly item. Piracy of Bath books was seldom a concern and only a few carry warnings that they have been registered at Stationers' Hall and that copyright infringements would be prosecuted. Yet some titles proved to be valuable commodities with a long, lucrative afterlife in reprints and new editions.*

Beneficiaries of a sustained national publishing boom and buoyed by the growth and prosperity of Bath itself, the leading Bath printers made a comfortable living, though constantly in competition for business among themselves. Set against other sectors of the local economy – building, clothes-making, shop-keeping, transport, the spa trade – the printing industry ranked as a small employer. Paid staff at all the printing offices, independent bookbinders, and engravers' shops combined, probably came to fewer than a hundred in 1800, though adding in apprentices and unpaid family helpers would swell the figure. Moreover they were the productive middlemen in a sometimes lengthy process in which the mechanical application of ink to paper was merely one stage. Far from working in isolation Bath's Georgian printers depended on a vast network of originators, distributors and consumers of print – not just in and around Bath, but regionally, nationally, and even beyond. A study of local printing and publishing therefore offers more than a slice of provincial business history. It opens up a larger field concerned with the making and transmission of knowledge, news, values, tastes, and ideas.

N.B. Illustrations in this book are not always reproduced at the exact size of the originals.

Setting the stage

Printing arrived at Bath surprisingly late – or perhaps not so surprisingly if we recall how small the early Georgian spa still was, with a resident population of only a few thousands and an economy largely sustained by summer visitors. London printers had begun moving into more populous English cities soon after the restrictive Licensing Act lapsed in 1695 and undertook not merely humdrum jobbing work but pamphlets, books and even newspapers. The first provincial newspaper indeed appeared at Norwich as early as 1701, quickly followed by others at Bristol, Exeter, and elsewhere. Bath by contrast had to wait until c.1729 for its first printer, and another fifteen years for a locally produced newspaper. It enjoyed the services of a bookseller from a much earlier date however. A succession of stationer/bookbinders known at Bath from 1610 onwards could doubtless have supplied books as well as stationery, if not always from stock then at least to order.

By the 1690s, the latest in that line, Henry Hammond, certainly called himself a bookseller and advertised novels, plays and maps besides such staples of the trade as stamped paper, parchment, ink, sealing wax, and proprietary medicines. He had also begun to ape the London booksellers by occasional forays into publishing, either at his own expense and risk (and retaining the copyright) or at the author's. Until Bath could support a reliable printer, the actual presswork was normally done in London or Bristol. In 1697 Hammond thus turned to a printer recently established at Bristol, William Bonny, to produce one of the earliest West Country printed books, the substantial 400-page *Bath Memoirs*, compiled by a Bath physician, Robert Peirce. Subsequently he seems to have preferred London printers even for the 24-page sermon by John Jackson, *Of God's Benefits to Mankind*, issued in 1707. The same year Hammond probably helped the elder Dr William Oliver publish his *Practical Dissertation on Bath Waters*, likewise in London, and he was certainly associated with a later edition. In 1717, once more under a London imprint, he brought out a pamphlet of English poetry translated into Latin by pupils of Bath Grammar School, and followed this in 1722 by joining a London bookseller to issue a new edition of Dr George Cheyne's influential *Essay on Gout*.

These metropolitan connections were further cemented when James Leake, himself a Londoner, took over Hammond's shop in 1722/23 and published several London-printed works in quick succession – George Cheyne's controversial *An Essay of Health and Long Life* (1724), Thomas Wynter's *Cyclus Metasyncritus* (1725), and *The English Instructor* by Henry Dixon, master of Bath's Bluecoats School (1727). This continuing predominance of London imprints does not mean of course that other Bath items, perhaps more ephemeral in character, had ceased to be printed in Bristol. An anonymous piece of light verse, *The Pleasures of the Bath*, is one example, printed by Samuel Farley at Bristol in 1721. Moreover it is likely that much of the commercial jobbing work for Bath customers – notices, trade cards, blank forms, ruled ledgers – would have been executed at nearby Bristol even if no examples from this period seem to have survived.

Once settled into his father-in-law's bookshop on Terrace Walk, the enterprising James Leake apportioned some of the space to a circulating library, one of the first in the country. Well-suited to a place like Bath where spa patients usually had ample opportunity for reading, such an institution was still a gamble. Despite a recent surge in visitor numbers the Bath season was quite short and still centred on the summer months, so Leake must have been banking on the custom of local gentry and professional men for the rest of the year. There were grounds for optimism. Bath was entering a new phase of population growth and investment. In 1727 the Avon Navigation opened up the river to traffic in heavy goods between Bristol and Bath, prompting a spate of residential building along the whole west side of the city. Scenting opportunity, the architect John Wood returned to his native Bath and was soon busy on Chandos Buildings, Queen Square, and Terrace Walk – where a second Assembly Rooms arose to meet an anticipated demand. Other speculative buildings were going up round the corner in Orange Grove. There was a buzz in the spa air. Maybe it was time at last for a printer to make his entrance?

The ELEMENTS of
CHRONOLOGY:
OR,
The CALENDAR Explained.

CONTAINING,

A DISCOURSE on the original Inftitution of the *Julian* and *Gregorian* Accounts of TIME: The Indiction of the *Romans*, and *Julian* Period: Of the Æra or Year of CHRIST: Of the Olympiads of the *Greeks:* Of the Building of *Rome:* And of the *Turks* and *Arabs* Account, &c.

The Movable and Fix'd FEASTS throughout the Year; the Cycles of the Sun, and Moon; the Epact; Golden Number; Dominical Letter; Key-Day; Number of Direction, &c. all largely accounted for.

Likewife complete TABLES for finding *EASTER,* according to the Rule of the *Nicene* Council.

WITH

An APPENDIX, *fhewing the moft plain and eafy* RULES *for* Menfuration *of* Superficies *and* Solids: *Alfo Arithmetical* ARCHITECTURE.

Together with various Ufeful TABLES.

All made Eafy to the meaneft CAPACITY.

By ROBERT SPURRELL,
Schoolmaster in Bath.

BATH: Printed by B. Lyons, for the Author

M.DCC.XXX.

Fig.1

The first Bath printer, B.Lyons, 1729-1730?

Of B.Lyons little is known, not even his full forename. What evidence there is shows he was working in Bath from 1729 until at least 1730 at a printing shop near the North Gate. No doubt the bulk of his output consisted of small-scale jobbing commissions – maybe tradesmen's bill-heads, public notices, prospectuses, official forms, and the like. One extant specimen of Lyons' printing is more substantial – a small book about the calendar system with various mathematical data, written by a Bath schoolmaster and printed in 1730. The title-page shown opposite below [Fig.1] is crowded with text and, typically for the period, seems to be laid out like a utilitarian handbill. Lyons has used a mix of five founts of roman type and one of italic, and within the book employs a decorative engraved headpiece and a woodcut initial as well [see below, Fig.2].

Hand printing was a laborious process, but presumably Lyons acted as his own compositor. Selecting from several different cases of type, he would accumulate text, character by character (letters, numerals, punctuation and spacers), first filling his composing stick and then transferring the justified lines of type to a galley to build into individual pages. For the actual printing he would have needed an assistant – see illustration opposite. The pages of solid type, locked in their correct imposition order into an iron frame, would be inked by the assistant wielding a pair of leather-covered ink-balls. Meanwhile, if Lyons was also his own main pressman, he fixed a sheet of dampened paper onto the tympan and hinged frisket, and folded it down over the bed of inked type. He next slid the moveable carriage that held the type until it came under the press's platen, and by pulling on a bar screwed the platen firmly down. This forced the paper to receive the impression of the inked type, but since it printed only one half of a sheet, the carriage would usually be run forward again in order to print the second half. The actions were then reversed. The printed sheet was added to the pile and the whole operation repeated with a fresh blank sheet. Some 100-200 sheets an hour could be run off in this manner, though each one generally had to pass through the press yet again to print the reverse side. Collating and folding the printed sheets came later after they had dried. Each copy of *The Elements of Chronology*, which made an octavo of 86 pages, required five-and-a-half sheets of paper printed on both sides. Calculated another way, it probably took the equivalent of an hour to print ten copies of the book.

During his brief professional stay Lyons printed several items for the flamboyant Thomas Goulding, Bath jeweller, militia captain, stager of events, and satirical author, who had already had the odd pamphlet and play printed in London before Lyons' arrival. It can be safely assumed that *A Poetical Account of the Rise and Progress of Tea* and a 4-page leaflet, *Captain Goulding's Advertisement*, were executed by Lyons in 1729, though neither carries his name. The 15-page *A Family Piece* does, however, and also supplies us with Lyons' address. In reality this pamphlet is merely the prospectus for a short octavo book with the same title that went to London for printing in late 1729 even though Lyons was still available. After 1730 and *The Elements of Chronology* though, Lyons is lost to view.

GENTLEMEN,

 Humbly presume to take this Opportunity of expressing my grateful Acknowledgment of the many Favours already received; and to request your Patronage and Protection of this small Treatise: Well knowing that Books have their Destinies from human Affections, Humours, &c. and are liked or disliked as the contrary Genius and different Dispositions of Men do lead them.

I am

Fig.2

A Farley interlude, c.1733-c.1741

How many months (or even years) elapsed between the departure of Lyons and the arrival of Felix Farley is unclear, but the latter had definitely opened a printing shop by 1733. A broadsheet he printed that year gave his address as outside the West Gate at the sign of the Shakespeare Head. The Farleys were a well-known family of West Country printers active in the region from as early as 1700 with printing shops over the next three decades at Exeter, Bristol, and Salisbury – places where they also started newspapers. Felix Farley's initial trial of Bath may have well been brief, however, because by 1734 he was running a Shakespeare Head printing office at Bristol. Here, three years later, his brother Samuel joined him. In 1739 a *Table of the Distances between the Principal Parts of... Bath*, a guide to the cost of a sedan fare ride, was printed by the Farley brothers at Bristol despite this being an obvious candidate for a Bath printer had there been one then. Yet two years later we find them executing a much more impressive piece of printing at Bath itself. The illustration below [Fig.3] shows a sample from John Wood's first publication, *The Origin of Building*, a handsome folio volume of over 240 pages with engraved plates. The actual printer may have been Samuel Farley alone, because that same year of 1741 his brother Felix returned to Exeter to revive the family newspaper there. The detail of the Farley brothers' movements is nevertheless complicated at this period, since they also kept their printing interest going at Bristol and had yet another concern at Pontypool in South Wales.

C H A P. IX.

Of the Temple, and the Parts thereunto belonging.

SOLOMON began this mighty Work, by enclosing Mount *Moriah* with a high *(a)* and stupendious Wall, built with Stones of such vast Magnitude that they were twenty *(b)* Cubits long, and six Cubits deep : This the King ordered to be done, that the Sides of the Hill might be so filled up to the Level of the Wall, as to form a spacious Area at Top, capable of containing the whole Structure, with its several *Courts*; and these Walls were made so strong, that the Fabrick above might stand upon Ground that would not yield to its incumbent Weight. Then *Solomon* erected the *Temple* in the following Manner, and according to the following Dimensions.

(d) 1 *Kings* vi. 1.
(e) *Acts* xiii. 18.
(f) 1 *Tim.* i. 4.

(a) *Jos. Ant.* l. 8. c. 2.
(b) Ib. l. 20. c. 8.

H h

THE

Fig.3

The début of Thomas Boddely, 1741-1743

For *The Origin of Building* the Farleys must have employed competent assistants. Might one of them have been Thomas Boddely, demonstrating his talents before establishing his own printing business in Kingsmead Street later that year? The proof that he was already operating independently before the end of 1741 lies in a dated handbill that he printed on behalf of John Wicksteed, its prominent heading echoing the sign board over Wicksteed's actual toyshop door in Orange Grove [Fig.4].

Stone Seals Engrav'd by
J. WICKSTEED, at his Machine
up Mr. *ALLEN*'s Road.

Fig.4

If Boddely *did* work on *The Origin of Building*, it might explain how he earned John Wood's approval to print his next book. Years later in 1755, soon after Wood's death, a rival printer (Stephen Martin) attacked Boddely for supposed ingratitude to Wood's memory, especially when it had been Wood's 'fatherly kind Protection, and liberal Assistance' that had rescued Boddely from remaining a mere printer's devil. A 'devil', Martin explained maliciously, 'is a Name given to the Most Menial Servant in the Printing Business, and such was Mr.B[oddely], when first taken Notice of by the late Mr.W[ood].' This statement cannot wholly be dismissed as hearsay because Martin had once served an apprenticeship to Boddely, but any rescue on Wood's part must surely have occurred well before the early 1740s when Boddely was no longer a lowly devil but an accomplished craftsman. All the same it was vastly encouraging that Wood should have entrusted him with his next book, *An Essay towards a Description of... Bath* [Figs.5-6 overleaf]. At the same time Wood changed his publisher. Instead of going back to the experienced James Leake who had handled *The Origin of Building*, he turned to Bath's second important bookseller, William Frederick in Orange Grove, another relative newcomer.

Although Wood's *Essay* was produced in octavo format, not folio, the types and the printing are sufficiently close to what appears in *The Origin of Building* to strengthen the idea that Boddely may have recently worked for the Farley brothers and even purchased some of their founts of type. From somewhere he also acquired a special rolling press for printing the thirteen fairly basic copperplate engravings by the London printseller John Pine and the more elaborate Van der Gucht portrait frontispiece [Fig.7 overleaf]. The entire work was intended to be completed in two parts, but in a note added at the end of part two Wood admitted he had wanted to include further sections on the government, trade and entertainments of Bath, but 'in this I am prevented from Want of Time'. Later in 1743 Boddely did in fact print a third part of the *Essay* containing this extra material together with a rather crude ground plan for Wood's intended Royal Forum. This third part is now exceedingly rare, though Bath Central Library holds one, possibly a proof. When the bookseller Frederick advertised the *Essay* in 1744 he spoke only of volumes 1 and 2, and by 1748 he had only copies of volume 2 left. By then John Wood was thinking of a new, enlarged edition, this time aimed at a wider readership, or so one must suppose from his forsaking both his local publisher Frederick and his local printer Boddely, and in 1749 bringing out a London edition with additional, better-quality engravings executed by Pierre Fourdrinier.

Between these two editions of the *Essay* came Wood's other Bath imprint, *A Description of the Exchange at Bristol*, dated 1745. No specific printer is named in the book, but we must assume it was Boddely, not just for typographical reasons but because he was the only Bath printer then in business – unless, as is sometimes claimed, Samuel Farley was still around. Limited to a print run of 300 copies, the majority of them subscribed for in advance of publication, this was the last of Wood's books to be printed at Bath. The rest were done in London or, in the case of his volume on Stonehenge, at Oxford.

A N
E S S A Y
Towards

A

DESCRIPTION
O F
B A T H,
And of the

BRITISH WORKS
I N I T S
Neighbourhood.

In TWO PARTS.

By *JOHN WOOD*, Architect.

B A T H:
Printed by THOMAS BODDELY.
1742.

Fig.5

The READER *is defir'd to make the following Cor-rections, and to amend any literal Faults he may meet with.*

PAGE 7. Line 23. for *of this* read *at this*; p. 8 . l. 25. r. *above* 600 *Years* ; p. 10. l. 4. for *the did* r. *he did* ; p. 16. l. 18. r. *to Hæmorrhages* ; p. 19. l. 9. for *which hath* r. *which have* ; p. 23. l. 7. for *and fqueezed* r. *fqueezed and dryed* ; p. 34. l. 14. for *Orchard* r. *Garden* ; p. 37. l. 28. for *Eaft-End,* r. *North-Eaft* ; p. 40. l. 11. r. CHAP. VII. p. 42. l. 27. r. *Meteora* ; p. 78. l. 1. r. 489 *Years after, &c.*

Fig.6

Fig.7

THE
BATH JOURNAL:

Printed and Publish'd by THOMAS BODDELY in BATH.

VOL. I.   MONDAY, *July* 16, 1744.   N° 21.

Wednesday's and *Thursday's* POSTS.
Arriv'd Two Mails from HOLLAND, *and Three from* FLANDERS.

CONSTANTINOPLE, [*one of the most famous Cities of Europe, the Middle of* Turkey, *and the Residence of the Grand Seignior, situated* 1570 *Miles from London*] *May* 27.

HE Porte is determined to prevent any Hostilities on the Coasts of its Dominions, by any of the European Powers at War; and it has thereupon been signified to all the Foreign Ministers here, that his Sublime Highness expects that, a Line being drawn from Sarta to Sidra, no Privateer shall presume to make any Capture within it. The News from Persia remains as uncertain as formerly, our Serafkier not being able to assemble an Army sufficient to act offensively; and Kouli-Kan being obliged to lay aside all Thoughts of attacking us, in order to compose some Troubles that are lately broke out in the Principality of Candahar.

Moscow, [*a great and rich City of* Russia] *June* 19. Lord Tyrawley has receiv'd fresh Orders from his Court, to hasten, as much as in him lies, the Departure of the Troops which her Imperial Majesty is engag'd to furnish the King of Great-Britain and the Queen of Hungary. The Affair of the Marquess de Botta is no longer talk'd of, and the Treaty of Alliance with the Court of Vienna is renew'd.

The Marquess de la Chetardie set out Yesterday from this City, in a very ill Humour. He made the utmost Efforts to obtain, first of all, an Audience of the Emperess; when he found that impracticable, he desired the Chamberlain, who brought the Order for his Departure.

HAMBOURG, [*a vast strong, large, and noble City of* Denmark] *July* 7. The Camp forming near Nieubourg, in the Electorate of Hanover, consists already of 10,000 Men : Some new Levies are expected there, and 'tis reckon'd this Camp will be 30,000 strong before the End of this Month.

The last Advices from Silesia say, that two Camps are mark'd out for the Prussian Troops, in the Neighbourhood of Neiss and Breslau.

From the Camp before Furnes, July 6. Marshal Saxe having within these few Days receiv'd a Reinforcement, his Army actually consists of 60,000 Men, and lies under Courtray. The Enemy are still at Oudenard, being 45,000 strong. The famous Partisan Folichini, who wears a Death's-Head on his Cap, has brought to M. Saxe's Camp 61 Hanoverians with their Horses, who were escorting a Convoy of Merchandize, valued at 400,000 Livres, with 10 Jesuits, twelve English Ladies richly dress'd, and a Box, wherein there was 22,000 Livres.

LISLE, [*a great, rich, and strong City and Castle of the Low-Countries, subject to the French*] *July* 11. M. d'Argenson no sooner heard, by an Express from the Count de Montal, that Prince Charles had passed the Rhine, but he went directly to inform the King of it : His Majesty seem'd at first to be not a little startled at it, but having heard the Letter read, he said, *There is certainly some Blunder here, and Montal is mistaken ; an Austrian Detachment may have passed the Rhine to allarm my Troops, but for the Queen's whole Army to have done it, is impossible.* Then the King called for Marshal Coigny's last Letter, and having read it, he said to M. d'Argenson, *Montal is mad, and Prince Charles too wise to hazard his whole Army.* His Majesty persisted in not believing this News, 'till six o'Clock in the Evening, when another Express arriv'd, dispatch'd by M. Coig-

cular, is a Mystery to us. Marshal Belleisle is expected every Hour on the Frontiers of Alsace, with the Van Guard of the Army.

From the LONDON GAZETTE,

COPY *of a Relation sent by his most Serene Highness Prince Charles, from his Head Quarters at Lauterbourg, the* 7th *of July,* 1744.

HIS most Serene Highness Prince Charles having detached Count Nadasti to make himself Master of the Town and of the Lines of Lauterbourg, this General thereupon, immediately after his Arrival, sent to summon the Town to surrender, which the Commandant having refused, Count Nadasti demanded of his Highness some Cannon and a Reinforcement, without which he could not succeed in taking the Lines. The Prince thereupon immediately sent the Prince of Wolfenbuttle and General Preising, with four Regiments of Foot and three of Horse, and marched with them himself; but scarce were they got Half-way, but the Town demanded to capitulate. This Post being of great Consequence, his most Serene Highness order'd, that the Capitulation should be granted, without standing upon Trifles; and it was accordingly signed, tho' the Garrison consisted of 1700 Men, and this Post might have held out ten Days. They engage not to serve against her Majesty the Queen, or her Allies, during one Year and a Day. As soon as his most Serene Highness arrived at Lauterbourg, he reinforced the 200 Men of the Regiment of Forgatsch, which General Nadasti had ordered to enter into it, to the Number of 800; and hearing that the Enemy was in March to gain the Lines on the Side of Weissenbourg, he detached General Nadasti towards that Town. His Highness being returned about Nine at Night to the Army, Advice came, that the main Body of the French and Bavarians was ranged in Order of Battle behind a Wood, ...

... Olive Oil.——*Harford* and *Coiswortby* 1167 Bar. of Belvidiere Raisins.——*Mich.* Atkins 32 Half-Chests of Soap.——*Corsley Rogers* 70 Ditto.——*One.* Tyndall and Comp. 100 Ditto, and 1 Box of Succads.——*John Dinwody* 1 But of Capers.——*Arth. Ballard* 6 Half-Chests of Sallad-Oil, 6 Half-Chests of Florence Wine.——*Richmond Day* 1 Half-Chest of Sallad-Oil.——*William Hart* 200 Marble paving Stones.——*Thomas Moore* 1 Marble Table.

In the ANTILOPE, Jo. Pitman, *Mast. from* Jamaica. Tho. Penington and Comp. 85 Hhds. 15 Tierces of Sugar, 285 Sticks of Lignumvitæ; 6 Hhds. Pimento.— Jos. Fitman 4 Hhds. of Sugar, 74 Sticks of Redwood, 18 Elephants Teeth, 1 Pipe of Madera Wine, 1 Bar. 1 Keg of Rum.—Arch. Douglas 17 Elephants Teeth.—Tho. Page 11 Ditto.—Michael Atkins 10 Hhds. of Ginger.—Henry Longe 1 Pipe Madera Wine.

In the SEAHORSE, John Hayles, *Mast. from* Virginia. John King and Co. 110 Hhds. Tobacco, 21 C. Staves

In the JOSEPH and MARY, Fra. Nich. Hugen, *Mast. from* Granville.

Step. Perry and Comp. 50 Tons Salt, 3 small Casks Brandy, 1 Hhd. 2 small Casks of Wine; *taken by the* King William *Privateer of Bristol.*

In the EBENEZER, M. Muller, *Mast. from* Christiana. Lewis and Parker, 76 C. Norway Deals, 11 C. half Deals, 2 C. Ufers, 4 C. Handspikes, 2 C. Battins, 1 Boom Spar.

PLANTATION-NEWS.

PHILADELPHIA, *March* 27. Last Tuesday arriv'd here Capt. Watkins, in 25 Days from Antigua, by whom we are inform'd, that the Lynn Man of War had taken two Spanish Privateers, in which was found a large Quantity of Money; also a Dutch Ship laden with a valuable Cargo from Old Spain, and has sent her unto Antigua. That Capt. Love, who was some Time since taken by the Dutch when he was Privateering from St. Kitt's, together with two Prizes he had taken, and was very ill used at Cur. cao, but since made Captain of a St. Kitt's Privateer that was lately in New-York, met with his own Sloop on the Spanish Main, which he retook, and soon after took a Spanish Privateer with 100 Men on board, great Part of whom enlisted with Capt. Love, and pilotted him in the Night into Laguira Harbour, where he cut out a Ship reckon'd the richest taken this War. Capt. Watson touched at Eustatia, where he was inform'd that they had ten Privateers belonging to St. Kitt's, and were fitting out four more; that they have had such prodigious Success that they flow in Money; and that a Division was lately made

BANKRUPTS. *William Kyte, of the City of* Oxford, *Innholder and Vintner.*——*Edward Hesking, of* Falmouth, *in* Cornwall, *Tobacconist and Chapman.*—— *Edward Tyler Lewes, of* Norwich, *Haberdasher and Chapman.*

DEATHS. *At his Seat at Baseldon near Reading in* Berkshire, *the Right Hon. the Lord Fane of the Kingdom of* Ireland : *He is succeeded in Honour and Estate by his only Son, the Hon. Charles Fane, Esq; Member of Parliament for* Tavistock *in* Devonshire.——*At* Hackney, Mrs. Phill, Relict of Mr. Phill, late an eminent Undertaker near the New-Church in the Strand : She has by her Will left the following Legacies, viz. 1000 l. to the Sons of the Clergy ; 100 l. to the Poor of Thame in Oxfordshire, where she was born ; 100 l. to the Poor of St. Mary le Strand, where she liv'd, and 50 l. to the Charity-School there ; 100 l. a Piece to all her poor Relations, which are numerous, and the Surplus to Mr. Wilson, an eminent Woollen-Draper in the Strand.*

MARRIAGES. *Mr. Allen, an Attorney in Good-man's-Fields, to Miss Fanny Huddlestone, only Daughter of the late Dr. Huddlestone, a beautiful young Lady with a Fortune of* 10,000 l.——*Alexander Philpot, Esq; to Miss Charlotte Barnard, Daughter of the late James Barnard of* Putney, *Esq; an agreeable young Lady with a Fortune of* 20,000 l.

Christnings and Burials in London this Week.

	Males—136		Males—158
Christened	Females 142	Buried	Females—181
	In all 278		In all 339

Decreas'd in the Burials this Week 19.

To be SOLD,
The BLACK-SWAN-INN,

In *Broad-Street*, BATH, With good Stabling, Coach-Houses, and a large Yard. *For further Particulars,* Enquire of Mrs. Chambers, next Door above the *Black-Swan* aforesaid ; or of Mr. *Sam. Purlewent,* Attorney.

To be SOLD,
In the Parish of CORSHAM, *in the County of* WILTS,

AN ESTATE, containing One Hundred and Forty-five Acres of Land, well situated, well wooded, and well watered, Tythe-Free ; an antient Mansion-House, with Barns, Stables, Out-Houses, and other Conveniencies, with pleasant Fish-ponds, contiguous Gardens, Orchards, &c. now in the Possession of John Handcock, Gentleman.——Particulars whereof may

The launch of the *Bath Journal*, 1744

Hitherto Bath had been reliant for news on the London press and on various regional organs such as the *Gloucester Journal* and the Bristol newspapers (run by the Farleys among others). By establishing the spa's own newspaper Boddely consolidated his position. But newspaper publishing did not in itself guarantee profits. Boddely sold his new journal at the normal price of 2d. per copy. Of this a ha'penny (½d.) would go on government excise duty, payable under the 1725 Stamp Act, and another farthing or so (¼d.) on each half-sheet of stamped paper, London-supplied, that he was legally obliged to use. The residue of 1¼d. had to cover all his expenditure on printing and distribution, including the wages of his printing staff and newsmen, payments to a network of provincial agents, and all his rent and overheads. Advertisements did produce some extra revenue, but half of the two shillings he charged for every advertisement inserted had to be surrendered in government tax.

Regular expenditure on London newspapers caused further outlay. One of the main services of the provincial press was to offer its readers a weekly digest of metropolitan journalism, and Boddely duly scoured the official *London Gazette* and fourteen other named London papers (plus some privately circulated manuscript newsletters) for newsworthy items. His sources covered a spectrum of political opinion, but Boddely wisely strove for neutrality. To be obviously partisan risked alienating readers, and to print outright criticism of government could be positively dangerous – as he well knew from the examples of Edward Farley, who died in gaol in 1728, and Samuel Farley, nearly prosecuted in 1731. Political comment was stifled anyway by the ban on direct reporting of parliamentary debates, with the result that domestic news tended to be duller reading than dispatches from abroad telling of military engagements and foreign intrigues. Boddely showed lucky timing, though, in launching his paper in 1744 just as the Jacobite rebellion began to build on the home front, creating a voracious public appetite for news. Compare 1752, for example, when Boddely complained openly of 'the great Dearth of News, and the little Expectations of a War, which is the Fund for News-Writers'. Not only was the 1744 news more stimulating, it arrived faster thanks to improved postal services, among them Ralph Allen's new Bristol-Bath-Salisbury cross-post.

The *Bath Journal* first appeared on Monday 27 February 1744, doubtless after much preliminary canvassing around Bath to obtain a sufficient number of subscribers. Like other provincial newspapers it was a weekly, printed on both sides of a large half-sheet and folded once to make four pages. The lay-out was sober enough: a three-column grid, simple title, space-saving type with considerable use of italic, and little in the way of decoration – though woodcut initials and other pictorial elements were gradually introduced. Instead of being printed at one go, the pages were made up and run off on different days as fresh material arrived in the post – pages 1 and 4 first, then 2, and finally 3 containing the most up-to-date 'intelligence'. Publication day was Monday, when Boddely's newsmen set out on their country rounds, carrying not only the *Bath Journal* but other items that Boddely printed or dealt in, such as pamphlets, Newbery's pocket books for children, and sundry proprietary medicines (like the much-touted Daffy's Elixir). Scarcely any local news was reported, whereas a growing proportion of the advertisements, often laid out like miniature handbills, were indeed to do with local sales and events. Room was usually made too for more diverting matter, poems, puzzles, extracts from other publications, and sometimes a reader's letter.

At a guess, Boddely would have started by printing several hundred copies, enlarging his output as demand grew. Many copies, including those taken by coffee houses and inns, must have passed from hand to hand and been seen even by casual readers. Catering to an increasingly literate public, newspapers informed, educated, spread fashions, moulded opinion, stimulated conversation, and of course entertained. Boddely and at least some of his subscribers saw the *Bath Journal* not as a mere ephemeral print but as a permanent record of events. For this reason he took the trouble to produce an annual volume index and a binder's title-page, and on one occasion even offered readers spare copies of back issues to complete their sets. There is no knowing whether it made much profit, especially considering the risks attached to credit arrangements with country subscribers. Conducting a provincial newspaper moreover required judgment, organisational skills, and constant attention to business every week of the year. On the other hand it raised Boddely's reputation and no doubt won him commissions to print other things besides.

JOHN DAVIS,

JEWELLER and GOLDSMITH,

ON THE

Lower-Walks, fronting the *North-Parade,* BATH,

MAKES, MENDS, and SELLS

Diamond, 𝕸ourning, and Fancy

RINGS, STONE-BUCKLES, STAY-HOOKS, SEALS,
and EGRETS for the Hair,

NECKLACES and EAR-RINGS,

In French Pafte or Scotch Pebbles:

And all SORTS of

Jeweller's Work,

After the Neatest and Newest Fafhions.

Likewife great Variety of

Gold, Silver and other Sorts of TOYS,

Silver and Pinchbeck Buckles; Snuff-Boxes; Writing-Boxes; Pocket-Books;
Toothpic Cafes; Pocket Tweezer-Cafes; Tea-Chefts; Smell Bottles; Cellars
of Bottles; Cafes of Silver or China-Handle Knives and Forks; India, Birmingham, or Pontipool Ware, in Dreffing Sets; Tea-Tables, Waiters, &c.

The Beft ENGLISH

TEA-KETTLES, LAMPS, and COFFEE-POTS,

USEFUL and ORNAMENTAL

CHINA-WARE,

And various other GOODS, *too numerous too infert.*

§†§ MONEY for OLD GOLD, SILVER and JEWELS.

☞ BATH: Printed by T. BODDELY,

Fig.9

Thomas Boddely and Jacob Skinner, 1745-1755

Proprietor, editor, and printer of the *Bath Journal*, Boddely had no rival for the next ten years except in copperplate printing, the line of business that Jacob Skinner followed. Skinner had secured a foothold at Bath earlier than Boddely. He was already taking on apprentices in 1737 (Nicholas Tucker) and 1738 (William Hibbert), and in the latter year was made an honorary freeman of Bath as reward for engraving the gold and silver boxes presented to the Prince of Wales' party during their Bath visit. But while he accepted other Corporation commissions at times (e.g. for engraved rings and brass badges), his forte lay in decorative printed design, elegant rococo trade cards, coats-of-arms, and private book-plates such as this one of 1751 devised for the budding Bath physician William Oliver [Fig.10].

Fig.10

It appears that Boddely too coveted this kind of superior jobbing work. In the end, fully nine months before Skinner's death in November 1754, he announced that he had installed a rolling press and could now execute heraldry, shopkeepers' bills, and other kinds of intaglio jobs. Presumably he had not kept the previous rolling press he owned in 1742.

All the same his everyday printing press (or presses) can seldom have been idle. The *Bath Journal* alone kept the pressmen occupied several times a week, and a hint of the jobbing activity may be gathered from occasional surviving examples like *The Oath of a Freeman* (a broadsheet for pinning on a wall*)* or the jeweller/goldsmith's trade-card reproduced opposite [Fig.9]. Among his output of 16-to-32-page pamphlets were charity and fast-day sermons, *The Twenty-Five Songs of Robin Hood*, and *A Disswasive from Lying* penned by the master of the Bluecoats School, Henry Dixon. On his own initiative Boddely produced an early local guidebook as well. Originally titled *The Tradesman's and Traveller's Companion*, this first appeared in 1745 and went through two further editions by 1753 when it became *The Bath and Bristol Guide*. And other book-length works issued under the firm's name included Samuel Bowden's *Poems on Serious Subjects* (1754), whose 422 pages contained much prose besides, and three medical treatises by Bath practitioners, David Hartley on operating for bladder stones (1746), William Oliver on warm bathing for gout (1751, 2nd ed. 1753), and Rice Charleton with his analysis of the mineral waters (1753).

THE

[N° 24]

BATH  Advertiſer.

By STEPHEN MARTIN.

SATURDAY, March 27, 1756.

On TASTE.

Not for himſelf he ſees, or hears, or eats,
Artiſts muſt chooſe his Pictures, Muſic, Meats. POPE.

WHAT we underſtand by Taſte is the peculiar Reliſh, that we feel for an agreeable Object, it ſhould always he founded on Truth ; but is often found the Child of Opinion only. True Taſte requires Toil and Study, which is the Reaſon why a falſe one is ſo apt to prevail : A good Taſte heightens every Science, and poliſhes every Virtue, is a Guide to Knowledge, and a Friend of Society : It enables us to diſtinguiſh Beauty and detect Error : In a Word, 'tis the Aſſemblage of all Propriety, and Centre of all that is amiable ; 'tis not confin'd only to Writings of every Kind, but regards Painting, Sculpture, and the whole Circle of Civility and Good-Manners : For Want of it Pertneſs paſſes for Wit, Dulneſs for Decorum, and Vanity for every Accompliſhment.

TASTE is moſtly uſed to expreſs a faſhionable Manner of Eating, and metaphorically for a faſhionable Manner of clothing the Body. If a Man would be well received in good Company, he muſt eat, though with Reluctance, according to the Laws eſtabliſhed by the laſt imported French Cook, and diſavow the native Reliſh of Good Engliſh BEEF and PUDDING.

THERE is a Fragment of *Athenæus*, in which he affirms, that Cooks were the firſt Kings, or chief Magiſtrates of the Earth, and that they obtained Sovereign Power, by forming Mankind into civil Societies ; which they effected by inſtituting ſet Meals, and dreſſing Meat in ſuch a Manner as rendered it moſt agreeable to every Man's Palate. 'Tis certain, the old Patriarchs, who, according to Sir *Robert Filmer*, muſt be reckoned Kings and Princes, were their own Cooks ; and one of their Number derived a Bleſſing to himſelf and his Poſterity, by making a ſavoury Haſh ; the Greek Commanders at the Siege of *Troy*, who were likewiſe all royal Sovereigns, never preſumed to ſet before their-Gueſts any Kind of Food not cook'd by their own Hands ; and *Achilles*, the greateſt Herb of them all, was famous for his Skill in broiling Beef-Steakes. In *Rome*, before their Principles were debauch'd, every Citizen, from the Dictator to the Plebeian, dreſſed his own Victuals ; and one of their greateſt Generals received the *Samnite* Ambaſſadors in a Room where himſelf was boiling Turnips for his Dinner ; and tho' they came to offer him a large Sum of Gold, their Meſſage did not interrupt his Cookery : Nay, among the Moderns, Cookery is in ſuch Repute, that the late Duke of *Orleans* (when Regent in the Minority of the preſent French King) had a Petit Cuiſine, to which (when tired with State-Affairs) he uſed to retire to recreate himſelf in dreſſing a Supper for his Friend and Miſtreſs. The Patriarchal and Conſular Cooks indeed never dreſſed above one Diſh at a Time, and that in a plain Manner ; but in Proceſs of Time, when the Luxury of the Table encreaſed, and it became faſhionable to multiply Diſhes, they required Aſſiſtants, and at length Cookery was exerciſed by hired Servants and Slaves only.

VANITY, and an Affectation of being eſteem'd Men of *Taſte*, is the Motive to the Profuſion, now a-Days, ſeen on Tables ; but, let ſuch know, eating itſelf ſeems rather a Subject of Humiliation than Pride, ſince the Imperfection of our Nature appears in the daily Neceſſity we lie under of recruiting it ; but the preſent Faſhion in eating ſeems rather deſtin'd to deſtroy than ſupport Nature : Chronical Diſtempers being the juſt Rewards of the preſent Manner of eating ; the Gout, Stone, Scurvy, Palſy, &c. being the never failing Attendants thereon : Animal Food is ſuppoſed to communicate its Qualities with its Nouriſhment ; in this Suppoſition it was that *Achilles* was nouriſhed with the Marrow of Lions, as Hiſtory ſays. If the Rule hold, as *Achilles* from hence commenced Hero, what muſt moſt of our preſent Gentry be eſteem'd, the principal Ingredients of whoſe Food is *Eſſence of Swine?*

IT may be objected, a grand Table is the Ornament of a great Fortune, which in ſome Senſe may be true : Hoſpitality is an ancient Virtue, and no where more remarkable than with the ancient *Britons*: But Hoſpitality is deſtroy'd by nice eating : Twenty Legs of Mutton would have made a Marriage Feaſt for our Anceſtors, but will now furniſh out but a ſmall Diſh : For the meer *Fruges conſumere nati* to eat thus is not a Wonder, but for Men of Senſe to fall into this Faſhion is ſurpriſing ; one would be almoſt tempted to think Fools had receiv'd this Method to bring them down to their Level ; for he who commonly feeds on *Spaniſh* Olives, *French* Ragoults ; or even an *Engliſh* Affects of *Pope's Eye* muſt talk Nonſenſe ;

---

for when a Company is thus gorged and glutted, there is not the leaſt Difference between the moſt ſtupid and the wittieſt Man in it.

What Life in all that ample Body, ſay
What heavenly Particle inſpires the Clay ?
The Soul ſubſides, and unwieldly inclines
To ſeem but mortal even in ſound Divines? POPE.

A DIALOGUE.

SAYS *Body* to *Mind*, 'tis amazing to ſee
We're ſo nearly related, yet never agree ;
But lead a moſt wrangling ſtrange ſort of a Life,
As great Plagues to each other as Huſband and Wife.
The Fault's all your own, with flagrant Oppreſſion,
Encroach ev'ry Day on my lawful Poſſeſſion :
The * beſt Room in my Houſe you have ſeiz'd for your own,
And turn'd the whole Tenement quite upſide down,
While you hourly call in a diſorderly Crew
Of vagabond † Rogues, who have nothing to do,
But run in and out, hurry ſcurry, and keep
Such a horrible Uproar, I can't get to ſleep.
There's my § Kitchen ſometimes is as empty as found,
I call for my ‖ Servants, not one to be found,
They all are ſent out on your Ladyſhip's Errand,
To fetch ſome more riotous Gueſts in, I warrant.
In ſhort, Things are growing I ſee worſe and worſe ;
I'm determin'd to force you to alter your Courſe. —
Poor *Mind*, who heard all with extreme Moderation,
Thought 'twas now Time to ſpeak, and make her Accuſation,
This I who, methinks, have moſt Cauſe to complain,
For I'm crampt and confin'd like a Slave in a Chain ;
I did but ſtep out on ſome weighty Affairs,
To viſit (laſt Night) my good Friends in the Stars,
But before I was got half as high as the Moon,
You diſpatch'd *Spleen* and *Vapours* to hurry me down ;
Vi & armis they ſeiz'd me, in the midſt of my Flight,
And ſhut me in Caverns as dark as the Night.
—'Twas no more (replied *Body*) than what you deſerv'd,
While you rambled abroad, I at Home was half ſtarv'd ;
And unleſs I had cloſely confin'd you in Hold,
You'd have left me to periſh with Hunger and Cold.
Mind.] I've a ‡ Friend in reſerve who tho' flow is yet ſure,
And will rid me at laſt of your inſolent Pow'r ;
Shall knock down your Mud Walls, the whole Fabric demoliſh,
And at once your ſtrong Holds and my Slav'ry aboliſh ;
And while in the Duſt your dull Ruins decay,
I ſhall ſnap off my Chains and fly freely away.

* The HEAD. † The THOUGHTS. § The STOMACH.
‖ The SPIRITS. ‡ DEATH.

Sunday and Monday's POSTS.

EUROPEAN INTELLIGENCE.

Portugal.

LISBON, [850 *Miles South-weſt of London*] *Feb.* 13.

THE 9th Inſt. we had an Earthquake which laſted ſix or ſeven Minutes, and few Days paſs away without feeling ſome Shocks more or leſs violent : So that we are ſtill in an alarming and deſolate Situation. The Monks and Nuns remain without Confeſſores, as the other Inhabitants do without Houſes. Four Regiments of Infantry and one of Dragoons are opening Roads through the Ruins of the City. This Week 230 Proſtitutes were taken up by Order of the Cardinal-Patriarch ; and Yeſterday 24 young Men were committed to Priſon, in order to oblige them to marry Girls whom they have debauched during our Calamities. An Order is iſſued for three great Families to depart from hence, one of whom was in pretty good Credit with the King ; and his Majeſty has aſſigned 100,000 Rees per Month for his Subſiſtence.

Spain.

MADRID, [800 *Miles South-weſt of London*] *Feb.* 24. Eight Men of War are fitting out at Ferrol to replace the like Number which are expected from the Weſt-Indies. The continual Drought for ſome Months paſt hath done conſiderable Damage in Valencia and other Provinces, and gives too much

---

Reaſon to apprehend that our next Harveſt will be as bad as the two laſt.

Italy.

NAPLES, [*the Capital of the Kingdom of Naples*] *Feb.* 24. As our laſt Advices from Madrid aſſure that the King of Spain is determined to obſerve a ſtrict Neutrality in the Broils between France and England, it is no longer a Doubt that our Court will do the ſame.

United Provinces.

AMSTERDAM, [*the Capital of the United Netherlands, on the River Amſtel, and the Sea call'd the Wey, a little to the Eaſtward of the Zuyder-Sea, 200 Miles and upwards E. of London*] *March.* 13. Letters from Smyrna, dated Jan. 21. adviſe, that the Plague was entirely ceaſed, and that Letters of Health had accordingly been given to ſeveral of our Merchant-Ships that were preparing to ſail from thence.

HAGUE, [*a Town of the United Provinces, two Miles Eaſt of the Sea, eſteemed a Village, but one of the largeſt and moſt elegant in Europe*] *March* 6. Since the Arrival of the Engliſh Tranſports in the Meuſe, Mr. Yorke hath received Orders from his Court to inſiſt upon the ſpeedy Embarkation of the 6000 Men demanded by his Maſter. It is ſo clearly expreſſed in the Treaty, that either of the Powers being barely threatened with an attack is a ſufficient Ground to demanded the ſtipulated Succours from the other, that there can be no Difficulty on this Head. Accordingly it has been obſerved to the Regents and Members of the State, that the French King having made himſelf Maſter of the Netherlands after the Death of Charles II. and being buſied in making ſuch Preparations on the Frontier as gave Umbrage to the Republic ; M. de Gelbie Malſon, their High Mightineſſes' Envoy at London, preſented, on the 1ſt of March 1701, a Memorial, deſiring his Britannic Majeſty to give Orders for holding the Succours ſtipulated by Treaty in Readineſs, that their High Mightineſſes might depend upon them in Caſe of Need, alledging that they were in great Danger of being attacked : That in the beginning of April the ſame Year, the States General again preſſed the King to grant the ſtipulated Succours : And that on the 13th of April the Houſe of Commons preſented an Addreſs to his Majeſty, that he would be pleaſed to fulfil the Treaty made with the States on the 3d of March 1677-8, and that the Houſe would enable him to do it effectually : That on the 13th of May the States-General wrote again to his Majeſty to repreſent to him their abſolute Need of Aſſiſtance to prevent their immediate Ruin ; and that in Conſequence of thoſe Repreſentations, the Succours demanded were ſoon after ſent to Holland, about a Year before the Maritime Powers declared War againſt France.

But all this ſuppoſes the Exiſtence of the *Caſus fœderis*, that is, that the Engliſh are not the Aggreſſors. The Provinces not being yet agreed on this Head, the States General are, and will long be, unable to give Colonel Yorke a favourable Anſwer to his Demand. In the mean Time the French Miniſters are not ſparing of their Menaces in their Remonſtrances ; but openly declare, that the King their Maſter will not ſee with Indifference the Republic ſending Troops to his Enemy.

Germany.

BRUNSWICK, *March* 6. The Marriage of the Princeſs Ann Amelia, ſecond Daughter of the Duke our Sovereign, to the Duke of Saxe-Weimar, is to be celebrated the 18th Inſt. on which Account that Prince has been here ſome Time.

Low Countries.

BRUSSELS, [*the Capital of the Province of Brabant, and of all the Auſtrian Netherlands*] *March* 11. According to Letters from Normandy moſt of the Regiments of Foot are arriv'd at the Quarters aſſigned them along the Coaſts of that Province. It is computed that there are at preſent 130 Fiſhing Veſſels and Merchantmen in the Port of Dieppe.

London, March 20.

The following Piece is a Copy of the Reply of the Court of France to the Anſwer of the States-General, to the Memorial made to them by the Marquis de Bonnac and the Count d'Affry, the 31ſt of December laſt.

The King has conſidered, with the moſt ſerious Attention the Anſwer returned by Order of the States General, in reference on the 9th of this Inſtant, to the Count d'Affry, Miniſter Plenipotentiary to their Republic.

20 2

Fig.11

Stephen Martin, John Keene, Samuel Farley II: journalism 1755-1759

The challenge to Boddely's monopoly eventually arrived not from outside but from his ex-apprentice, Stephen Martin, first indentured in 1747 and hence only a young ex-journeyman when in 1755 he bought new type and opened a printing shop at the 'Brick House', just outside the West Gate quite close to Boddely's 'Pope's Head' press in Kingsmead Street. Not content with competing for jobbing and book printing, Martin made the rivalry acutely personal by starting up a newspaper, the *Bath Advertiser*, first issued on 18 October 1755. Its very name showed an intention of tapping the potentially lucrative publicity market, even though it would take time to build an adequate subscription base to satisfy would-be advertisers of the paper's wide distribution. Declarations that advertisements would be received by agents at Exeter, Dorchester, Salisbury, and other far-flung places indicated Martin's ambition in this regard. The *Bath Advertiser* was a general weekly, however, containing a proper quotient of domestic and foreign news, literary items, and the like. Bearing the city arms in the heading the publication was neatly laid out and aped the recent practice of the *Bath Journal* in its use of double rules to organise the page.

Thomas Boddely seemingly continued to prosper and, as an active freemason, became Master of the Bear Lodge in December 1755. Before completing his six-month turn of duty, however, he died, probably rather suddenly, on 9 June 1756 leaving a void to be filled. With a successful newspaper at stake, his family acted at once. Boddely's brother-in-law, John Keene, though apparently no printer himself, took over the business – with, as he stated, 'proper assistance' – and he emphasised continuity by renaming the newspaper *Boddely's Bath Journal* from the issue of 14 June. This change of title failed all the same to deter Samuel Farley II, son of the Felix Farley who had printed at Bath in the 1730s, from embarking on yet another journalistic venture, *Farley's Bath Journal*. It was short-lived. Printed from an address in Bath Marketplace and linked to two rival *Bristol Journals,* it made a little noise in September/October 1756 and then disappeared. Only two issues are definitely extant dated 11 and 18 October. The size and commercial importance of Bath were expanding all the while, but there was still a question whether the spa could support more than two viable newspapers at any one time.

In any case, making profits through newspapers soon became a dubious proposition anywhere. The 1757 Stamp Act raised the duty on a half-sheet of letterpress paper by a ha'penny (½d.) and doubled the tax on advertisements to two shillings, so upping the cost of inserting an advertisement to a punitive four shillings a time. Besides the likely loss of advertising and subscription revenue, it meant that newspapers faced additional pressure on cash flow because taxes had to be paid at once, whereas subscribers paid in arrears. No wonder that John Keene, like other proprietors, complained bitterly at the injustice. Stephen Martin told his *Bath Advertiser* readers that the measure was an 'extraordinary additional Clog on the Liberty of the Press' and that newspaper printers were perhaps the only 'Artists' obliged to pay two-thirds of their receipts to the government.

One result of financial stringency must have been a fiercer struggle for customers, and here the question of up-to-date news coverage had some importance. The *Bath Journal* liked to stress its currency. Coming out on Monday, it probably printed page 1 (summarising Thursday's London post) on the Thursday or Friday, pages 2-3 on the Saturday, and page 4 – largely made up in advance – on the Monday after receiving the latest *Daily Gazette* from the capital. Any important last-minute news could be accommodated by removing advertisements, especially the *Journal*'s own page 4 notices. The *Bath Advertiser* doubtless followed a similar but earlier printing cycle and naturally made the counterclaim that its Saturday publication date gave it the advantage. It also boasted about its wide circulation covering Reading to south Somerset, and took special pleasure in taunting the Bristol press over its commercial success on their home ground. Indeed the *Advertiser* maintained a good reputation in the region through five full years before a fresh competitor arrived on the scene.

Book production around 1760

Both Keene and Martin took on any printing jobs that came their way, but only odd examples of what may well have been a large production of handbills and other ephemera have survived. We know, for instance, that Martin printed Corporation bylaws to serve as public notices, that printed handbills were regularly tacked up in the Pump Room and coffee houses, and that fly posting on Bath buildings was a nuisance at times. Pamphlets and books have better escaped oblivion, either as actual physical specimens or through contemporary references in print. Among Martin's output at this period were a rogue's history (*The Life of William Williams...* [with an] *Account of his Execution*, 1755), a volume of English and Latin verse (Thomas Hull, *A Collection of Poems and Translations...*, 1756, 2nd ed. 1759), a medical report (William Oliver, *Cases of Persons admitted into the Infirmary at Bath*, 1760), and the schoolbook illustrated below [Fig.12] (*Directions to Young Scholars for Translating Latin...*, 1757). John Keene meanwhile brought out a fourth edition of the *Bath and Bristol Guide* c.1759, as well as printing several other titles, including an anonymous poem, in English and Latin, shown on the opposite page [Fig.13]. Nevertheless there was no obvious preference given to Bath printers even when the city booksellers Leake and Frederick were (singly or jointly) concerned in a particular publication. Commissions continued to go to printers in London or perhaps to Bristol. One such example was *A Treatise on the Medicinal Qualities of Bath Waters*, a substantial 300-page volume by a Bath physician, J.N.Stevens, co-operatively published by Leake, Frederick, and three London booksellers, and printed at Bristol in 1758 by Elizabeth Farley, Felix Farley's widow.

22   *Directions to Young Scholars, &c.*

RULE II.

This Word *of*, coming after a Verb is made by a Prepofition.

EXCEPTIONS.

1. After *panitet, pudet, tædet, piget, miferet* and *miferefcit*, it is a Sign of the Genitive.
2. After Verbs of accufing, condemning, warning, or abfolving, it is a Sign of the Genitive or Ablative.
3. After the Verb *fum* fignifying a Property or Duty, it is a Sign of the Genitive.
4. After Verbs of depriving and unloading it is a Sign of an Ablative.
5. After Participles of the Preter-Tenfe and Future in *dus*, it is a Sign of the Dative or Ablative with a Prepofition.

RULE III.

At or *in* coming before the Name of a City or Town being of the fingular Number, and firft and fecond Declenfion, are Signs of the Genitive Cafe; but if the Word be of the third Declenfion, or Plural Number, are Signs of the Dative or Ablative.

How to know the Dative *Cafe.*

RULE I.

The Noun which hath *to* before it, is ufually the Dative Cafe.

EXCEPTION.

To after thefe Verbs *attinet, pertinet, fpeetat, loquor, hortor, invito, provoco,* and Verbs of Motion, is made by the Accufative Cafe with *ad.*

How

Directions to Young Scholars, &c.   23

How to know the Accufative *Cafe.*

RULE I.

The Word coming next after the Verb, without any Sign before it, anfwering to the Queftion *whom* or *what*, is the Accufative Cafe.

EXCEPTIONS.

1. After Verbs Subftantives, Paffives, or of Gefture, it is the Nominative Cafe.
2. After *mifereor, miferefco*, the Genitive.
3. After *reminifcor, oblivifcor, recordor,* and *memini*, Genitive or Accufative.
4. After *Interest* and *Refert* the Genitive; unlefs in thefe Words, *me, thee, his, us, you, whom*, which are made by the Ablative, Poffeffive, Feminine, *meâ, tuâ, fuâ, noftrâ, veftrâ, cujâ.*
5. After Verbs fignifying Profit, Difprofit, Help, Favour, obeying, refifting, ferving, trufting, or believing, it is made by the Dative.
6. So alfo after thefe Verbs, *pareo, placeo, difpliceo, patrocinor, medeor, libet, indulgeo, ftudeo, doleo,* and *blandior* it is a Dative.
7. After the Compounds of *fum* except *Poffum*, a Dative.
8. After Verbs of threatning, commanding, pardoning, the Words fignifying the Perfon is ufed in the Dative Cafe.
9. After Verbs of wanting and *potior*, it is made by the Genitive or Ablative.
10. After *fungor, fruor, utor, lætor, glorior, muto, dignor, vefcor, gaudeo, fuperfedeo, numero, communico,* it is the Ablative Cafe.
11. After *fto* and *confto* fignifying to coft, and *valeo* to be worth, the Word fignifying the Price, is the Ablative. Except thefe Genitives put fubftantively, *tanti, quanti, pluris, minoris.*

RULE

Fig.12

[1]

✥✥✥✥✥✥✥✥✥✥✥✥✥✥✥✥✥✥✥✥✥✥✥✥✥✥✥✥✥✥✥✥✥✥✥✥✥✥

PRÆ-EXISTENCE:

A

P O E M.

_____

NOW had th' *Archangel* trumpet, rais'd fublime
    Above the walls of *Heaven*, begun to found;
All *Æther* took the blaft, and *Hell* beneath
Shook with celeftial noife; th' Almighty *Hoft*
Hot with purfuit, and reaking with the blood
Of guilty *Cherubs* fmeared in fulphurous duft,
Paufe at the known command, of founding gold.
And firft they clofe the wide *Tartarian* gates,
Th' impenetrable folds on brazen hinge
Rowl creaking horrible, The din beneath
O'ercomes the roar of flames, and deafens *Hell*;
Then through the folid gloom with nimble wing
They cut their fhining traces up to light;
Return'd upon the edge of heavenly day,
Where thinneft beams play round the vaft obfcure,

And

Fig.13

[45]

[Nº. 12.] The Bath Chronicle [Vol. 1.]

AND

Weekly GAZETTE.

[Price Two-Pence Halfpenny.]

Printed and publish'd by C. POPE, and Cº. at the Printing-Office in STALL-STREET : Where PRINTING in all its Branches is perform'd on the moſt reaſonable Terms, and in the neateſt Manner.

[*The above C. POPE ſerv'd his Apprenticeſhip with the late Mr. BODDELY, and has had the ſole Management of the Bath Journal for theſe laſt five Years.*]

THURSDAY, JANUARY 1, 1761.

To the PRINTER of the
Bath Chronicle and Weekly Gazette.

SIR, BATH, Dec. 29, 1760.

As you declar'd in your Proposals, that your Paper was calculated for general Entertainment and Inſtruction ; and that you wou'd always pay a proper Regard to ſuch uſeful Hints as might be communicated to you by your Correſpondents ;—I make no Doubt but you will inſert what I herewith ſend.

A SHORT DISCOURSE on
CHRISTMAS-DAY, or the Nativity of
our bleſſed Saviour *Jeſus Chriſt.*

A SHORT DISCOURSE on
NEW-YEAR's DAY : Or, The
Circumciſion of CHRIST.

WE celebrate this Feaſt in Memory of our Lord's Circumciſion.

Two COMMON CHARACTERS.

FANNY is beautiful and young,
And wants no Inclination ;
Her Virtue weak, her Paſſion ſtrong,
But fears her Reputation.

Fig.14

Pope, Keene and Martin, 1760

Like Stephen Martin, Cornelius Pope had served his apprenticeship to the printing trade with Boddely. Under Boddely's successor John Keene, he was sole manager of the *Bath Journal* and in effect ran the whole business (sited at the 'Pope's Head'!) – even to the extent, as Keene later alleged, of printing off handbills and trade cards on his own account and without Keene's authorisation. In October 1760, now richly experienced, Pope took flight with his own newspaper, the *Bath Chronicle.* This was less a snub to his erstwhile employer, Keene, than a confrontation with Stephen Martin and the *Bath Advertiser,* which was just completing its fifth year of publication and marking the event with a quinquennial index. The *Advertiser*'s management (Stephen Martin senior and junior) retaliated on the spot by announcing that from now on they would re-name their own paper the *Bath Chronicle* and switch their day of publication from Saturday to Thursday, the very title and the very day that Pope himself had chosen. This act of piracy, Pope's own metaphor for it, was clearly designed to sow confusion in customers' minds, even if the two papers did bear different subtitles – *Universal Register* for Martin's, *General Advertiser* for Pope's. The two *Bath Chronicles* emerged simultaneously therefore on 16 October 1760 and the battle for supremacy began. Pope's newspaper, with its black-letter heading and tightly packed four-column display, in time gained the upper hand and forged a lasting reputation. Despite this, Martin's paper continued to appear – from 1763 under the name of *Martin's Bath Chronicle.* Martin himself kept going at least until 1764 [Fig.15 below] and was succeeded by M[ary?] Martin, most likely his widow, who was still printing as late as 1779.

P O E M S

On various SUBJECTS,

Divine, *Moral* and *Entertaining:*

T H E

POSTHUMOUS WORKS

O F

Mr. *JACOB AXFORD,*

OF THE CITY OF BATH,

Late Surgeon of his Majefty's Ship, Scipio;

Written for his own AMUSEMENT.

✳✳✳✳✳✳✳✳✳✳✳✳✳✳✳✳✳✳✳✳✳✳✳✳✳✳✳✳✳✳

B A T H:

Printed by S. MARTIN, juft without WEST-GATE.

―――――

MDCCLXIV.

Fig.15

Cornelius Pope and Sarah Fielding's *Xenophon*

Pope's ground-floor printing office on the east side of busy Stall Street, not far from the Pump Room, occupied a central location convenient for a general printer and for the multifarious business of running a newspaper. Here in spring 1761, following the death of Bath's celebrated master-of-ceremonies, he printed an 8-page Latin *Epitaphium* on Richard 'Beau' Nash, and a year later included a frontispiece portrait of Nash in the first edition of *The New Bath Guide* [Fig.16]. This latter item was a further bid for attention, the word 'new' in the title plainly declaring this was no tired version of the old Boddely guide that Keene had continued. Guidebooks were becoming a staple of local publishing as spa visitors arrived in ever-growing numbers, and over the next few years Pope brought out four more updated editions. Each time he preserved the made-up pages of type to save having to compose afresh with every new edition. For a small-format, 64-page publication this procedure did not lock up too much of his stock of types. Nor did printing the *Bath Chronicle* put a strain on his stock, since the type was distributed (i.e. returned to the cases, ready for re-use) after each weekly print-run. A full-scale book demanded greater resources, though, even if it were printed in stages as Pope's first substantial commission, *Xenophon's Life of Socrates*, probably was.

Fig.16

His client was Sarah Fielding, sister of the novelist Henry Fielding and a successful author in her own right. Moving to Bath in 1754 after her brother's death, she had remained as intellectually active as ever, regularly stimulated by the company of Sarah Scott, Elizabeth Montagu, Jane Collier, and other bluestocking friends. Her English translation of Xenophon [Fig.17] was a formidable achievement all the same, and she might have been expected to turn to an experienced London publisher rather than engage the youthful Cornelius Pope. But as she explained to her long-standing classics mentor,

James Harris, in April 1761, part of the book had already gone to press at Bath – 'for I could not undertake a Journey to London, and here is an ingenious young Man lately set up that I believe will do very well'. Although Pope apparently began printing the first sections that spring, the 380-page *Xenophon* did not finally appear until 1762. One likely cause of the delay may well have been the need to accumulate a respectable advance subscription list – that common, risk-limiting device for financing works of uncertain sales potential. Pope may indeed have printed a prospectus soliciting subscribers that Sarah Fielding then circulated to her acquaintance in Bath and beyond. A small sample of the very satisfactory list of 611 subscribers she succeeded in enrolling is reproduced below [Fig.18]. Even had the translation not received the critical acclaim it did on publication, at least all the expense of printing and distribution must have been more than covered.

(I)

XENOPHON's MEMOIRS

O F

SOCRATES.

BOOK I.

CHAP. I.

I HAVE often wondered by what Arguments the Accufers of SOCRATES could perfuade the Athenians that he had behaved in fuch a Manner towards the Republic, as to deferve Death : For the Accufation preferred againft him, was to this Effect :---

A   " SOCRATES

Fig.17

Rev. Dr. Taylor, Cann. Refid. of St. Paul
Tho. Towers, Efq.
Mrs. Mary Tonfon
John Tavers, Efq.
Mrs. Thompfon
Thomas Tyndall, Efq. King's-Proctor

V.

Rev. Mr. Viney
Mifs Vaughan
Arthur Vanfittart, Efq.
Mrs. Vernon
Mrs. Vincent

W.

Right Hon. the Countefs of Waldgrave
Right Hon. Vifcount Weymouth
Rt. Hon. Vifcountefs Weymouth
Right Hon. Lord Warkworth
Right Hon. Lady Frances Williams, 3 B.
Hon. Mrs. Wadman, 3 B.
*** WortleyMontagu, Efq. 4 B.
Rev. Dr. Wynne
William Whitehead, Efq.
Mrs. Walmfley
Mrs. Webb
Mrs. Wittington
John Wadman, Efq. 3 B.
Richard Warner, Efq.
Mifs Wray
**** Williams, Efq.
Mrs. Wollafton
Mrs. Wife
Matthew Wife, Efq.
Mr. Chriftopher Wright, Jun.
Wadham Wyndham, Efq.
Mrs. Wright

James Warren, Efq.
Mrs. Warburton
Mifs Worfen
Mrs. Willcox
Mr. Wills
Lewis Way, Efq.
Mrs. Williams
Rev. Mr. Wheatland
Dr. Thomas Wilfon, Refid. of St. Paul's
Mrs. Letitia Winftanley
Mrs. Dorothy Winftanley, 2 B.
Mifs Whitby
William Whitehead, Efq. 2 B.
Mrs. Wilmot
Mr. Wilcox, 6 B.
Mifs Wowen
Mr. Whitaker
John Woodward, Efq.
John Watts, Efq.
Mrs. Wilmot
Fowler Walker, Efq.
Rev. Mr. Woodroffe
Mr. John Wiltfhire
Mr. Walter Wiltfhire
Dr. WilliamWynne, Doct.Com.
Mrs. Webb
Mrs. Warburton
Rev. Mr. Jof. Warton, 2 B.
Rev. Mr. Thomas Warton
Mrs. Williamfon
*** Wake, Efq. Trin.Coll.Cam.
Mr. Wright
Richard Whitem, Efq.
Mr. Worley
John Waters, Efq.
Mifs Ward
Saunders Welch, Efq.
William Thomas Wifhart, Efq.

Fig.18

Pope, Archer and Keene

Publishing Sarah Fielding's *Xenophon* was a satisfying achievement but it led to fewer commissions from other Bath authors than Cornelius Pope might have expected. He did however print a number of shorter books in the mid-1760s, including *Cursory Remarks on Investigating the... Bath and Bristol... Waters* by the controversial apothecary Charles Lucas (1764) and a monograph on the virtues of castor oil by another medical man - Peter Canvane's *A Dissertation on the Oleum Palmae Christi...* (1766). Otherwise he executed routine jobbing orders – anything from a leather dresser's trade card to the catalogue of an exhibition of stuffed birds – and concentrated above all on the formidable task of editing, publishing and circulating the *Bath Chronicle* week in, week out. Having moved his printing office in late 1765 from Stall Street to roomier quarters in St James's Street opposite the church, Pope engaged a young assistant, William Archer, to manage the business, notwithstanding the fact that Archer was already running his own copperplate printing shop in Horse Street close by. Archer evidently combined the two tasks with some aplomb, because in summer 1768 Pope sold him his whole stock-and-trade, the *Chronicle* included, and a year later left Bath. Archer then transported his copperplate press to St James's Street, and immediately found time to print, or maybe to complete under his own name, a 255-page volume of verse (T.Underwood, *Poems*, 1768), of which a part page, with decorative tailpiece, is shown below [Fig.19]. Was all this an elaborate holding operation or did Archer almost at once find himself in financial straits? The truth is that within a mere eight weeks of succeeding Pope he had acquired an active partner in Richard Cruttwell, and *Archer's Bath Chronicle* had turned into the less personalised *Bath and Bristol Chronicle*. Meanwhile, a spectator to all this, John Keene went on producing the rival *Bath Journal*. He also busied himself with everyday jobs like printing the annual report of the Pauper charity [opposite Fig.20], but undertook relatively little book work. One notable exception was William Brimble's *Poems Attempted on Various Occasions*, printed in 1765 [opposite Fig.21].

198   M I S C E L L A N I E S.

Then, to whet for Dinner's Treat,

Numbers up the Hills you'll meet :

But, 'bove all, the Ev'ning's Sight,

Subject of extreme Delight,

At the brilliant, crouded Ball,

There collected, fee 'em all—

    Abruptly yours---my Paper checks ;

How cruel this !---my beft Refpects.

Fig.19

Receipts and Diſburſements

OF THE

PAUPER-SCHEME,

For the YEAR 1768.

BATH: Printed by J, KEENE.

Fig.20

[I]

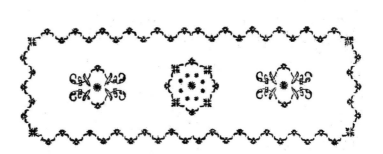

P O E M S

ON

Various OCCASIONS.

On ſeeing a Human Skeleton found with a Gold Ring, buried in a Stone Coffin.

ES, ſilent teacher! I the leſſon read,
And view the ſtate of all the mighty dead;
Stript of the glare with which thou doubt-
leſs ſhone,
Now ſcalpt thy ſkull, and ſkinleſs ev'ry bone;
With duſt coeval all to atoms turn'd;
What beautious thee, perhaps, once bright adorn'd:

Fig.21

B

The

A one-year partnership: Archer & Cruttwell, 1768-1769

Richard Cruttwell, only recently out of his apprenticeship to a London printer, may well have heard of the opportunity at Bath through his elder brother William Cruttwell, publisher of the *Sherborne and Dorset Journal*. A bequest from a great uncle enabled him to take a substantial share in the *Bath Chronicle* in late September 1768 and to buy out Archer altogether a year later having satisfied himself of the market. The omens looked good. Bath was undoubtedly fashionable and prosperous. Its high season now lasted from autumn round to spring, and it was expanding fast, as much in resident population and visitor numbers as in handsome new buildings and general amenities – not least among them the services of five or six booksellers and circulating libraries. These would be prime outlets for sales of *The Bath Contest* and its supplement *The Conciliade*, published by the Archer/Cruttwell partnership in spring 1769 and compiled from items already printed in the *Bath Chronicle*. It was really a chance too good to miss. Targeted especially at visitors, many of them actual participants in the story, the two modest octavos chronicled each event in the recent campaign to elect a new master of ceremonies on the death of the previous incumbent, Samuel Derrick. *The Bath Contest* [Figs.22-24] was worth buying for its frontispiece alone, a sharp visual comment on the fury of the battle, originally engraved for the *Oxford Journal*.

T H E

BATH CONTEST:

Being a COLLECTION of all the

PAPERS, ADVERTISEMENTS, &c.

Publifhed BEFORE and SINCE

The DEATH of Mr. DERRICK,

BY THE

CANDIDATES

For the OFFICE of

MASTER of the CEREMONIES,

And their FRIENDS,

DIGESTED IN REGULAR ORDER.

St. *George*'s Race with ftout St. *Patrick*'s vies ;
Warm as the Conteft, noble is the Prize,
The *Crown* of *Bath !*—What Empire can compare
With that o'er Men of Tafte, and Ladies fair ?

B A T H:

Printed and fold by ARCHER and CRUTTWELL,

In ST. JAMES'S-STREET,—*Price* ONE SHILLING.

Fig.22

Fig.23

THE BATH CONTEST. 51

under-named Noblemen and Gentlemen, or as many of them as will pleafe to attend on the Occafion, and I will abide by their Determination between Mr. PLOMER and me.

WILLIAM BRERETON.

Lord HUNTINGDON,   Mr. CALLIS,
Lord HEREFORD,   Mr. MARRIOT,
Lord SOMERVILLE,   General SANDFORD,
Sir GEORGE YOUNG,   Mr. NORRIS,
Sir W. St. QUINTIN, Mr. BATERSBY,
Col. SOMERVILLE,

SIR,   To Mr. BRERETON.

I Think it improper to accept of your Propofal, though I have the higheft Opinion of thofe honorable Gentlemen whofe Names you have mentioned in your Note.

I am, Sir, your humble Servant,

R. H. PLOMER.

P. S. I have already publicly made an Offer for the Sake of the Peace of the Community, which it becomes me to abide by.

MR. BRERETON immediately fent a Note to Mr. *Plomer*, defiring to know what Propofal he had made, as Mr. *Brereton* had not received any Propofal from Mr. *Plomer*: To which Note Mr. *Plomer* fent the following Anfwer.

SIR,   To Mr. BRERETON.

I Have already made a public Declaration, (not to you in particular) that I would for the Peace of this Community refign my Pretenfions, provided you would your's, unto a third Perfon that might be agreeable to the Company. You will obferve that your Son was then underftood to be excepted.

I am your humble Servant,

Bath, 5th April, 10 o'Clock.   R. H. PLOMER.

H

Fig.24

Fig.25

Fig.26

Frontispiece.

THE

GENUINE DISTRESSES

OF

DAMON and CELIA.

IN A

SERIES of LETTERS

BETWEEN

The LATE GENERAL CRAUFURD,

Sir JOHN HUSSEY DELAVAL, BART.

Sir FRANCIS BLAKE DELAVAL, K.B.

AND

TWO UNFORTUNATE LOVERS.

By WILLIAM RENWICK.

Notitiam primofque gradus vicinia fecit;
Tempore crevit amor.   OVID.

VOL. I.

BATH:

Printed by R. CRUTTWELL, for the AUTHOR;
And fold by Mr. DODSLEY, Pall-Mall; Mr. ALMON, Pic-
cadilly; Mr. GRIFFIN, Strand; Mr. F. NEWBERY,
Ludgate-Street; and Meffrs. RICHARDSON and
URQUHART, Royal Exchange, London.

M DCC LXXI

Fig.27

Richard Cruttwell, 1770-1774

No longer constrained by a partner, Cruttwell began to pay more attention to printing books. The financial and publishing arrangements varied in every case. Archer and Cruttwell together had published *The Bath Contest* at their own risk, and Cruttwell on his own sometimes did the same. Indeed *The Rival Ballrooms* (1774), another round-up of the printed exchanges on a contentious local issue, simply echoed the earlier publication. Other items were more utilitarian – abstracts of Acts of Parliament (in book or poster formats), *The House-keeper's Accompt Book* (a quarto first issued in its familiar blue covers for New Year 1773 and produced annually thereafter well into the nineteenth century), and a variety of three-penny sheets – tables of wheat prices, market regulations, postal services, and the like. Besides selling his wares at the printing office itself, Cruttwell made full use of his newsmen and retailing agents, who naturally also carried copies of *The [Entertaining] Miscellany,* an occasional supplement to the *Bath Chronicle* first issued in January 1772.

Self-published items nevertheless accounted for only a small percentage of Cruttwell's growing output. The bulk of his book printing was on behalf of others – either individual authors or bookseller/ publishers – and at their expense. Three examples of author-inspired imprints date from 1770, his first full year of independent operation – *Idalian Buds*, a collection of verse by F.J.Guion; *The Art of Dressing the Hair*, also in verse; and *The Life and Extraordinary Adventures... of Timothy Ginnadrake* (1770-2). The author of this latter rather anecdotal, three-volume autobiography was Francis Fleming, once the leading violinist in the Pump Room band. It was presumably he who paid personally for the frontispiece portraits inserted in volumes 1-2 [Figs.25-26 opposite]. The commercial success of these and other author-sponsored works can only be guessed at, though clearly *The Register of Folly, or Characters... at Bath and the Hot-Wells* (by 'An Invalid', perhaps Joseph Draper) proved a hit since it went through four editions in six years, 1773-9. The title-page of William Renwick's two-volume novel *Damon and Celia* [Fig.27 opposite] shows how bookseller support could often be mustered in advance of publication. In this instance five notable London booksellers were named, whereas with *Timothy Ginnadrake*, mentioned above, only one London bookseller was listed but five in Bath.

Alternatively, a book's sales potential might persuade a bookseller or a consortium to cover production costs themselves, possibly with certain guarantees from the author. Cruttwell executed many books of this character. The annual *New Bath Guide* was thus printed from 1770 onwards for the Bath bookseller William Taylor. Other printing commissions at this period were undertaken for such well-known London bookseller/publishers as J.Lowndes (i.e. *An Essay on the Bath Waters*, 2 volumes, 1770-2, by the up-and-coming Bath physician William Falconer), W.Griffin (*The Rival Beauties*, partly by R.B. Sheridan, 1772, 2ⁿᵈ ed. 1773), and E. & C.Dilly (*A Modest Plea for the Property of Copyright,* 1774, by the reputed historian Catharine Macaulay, then living at Bath).

Printing substantial books demanded a good stock of type. Cruttwell seems to have been adequately supplied with roman founts, but still lacked anything more exotic when in 1774 he required large upper-case Greek letters for the title of Ralph Schomberg's *Mousike-Iatreia.* Luckily he could just get by with the roman alphabet, and by contriving a Greek sigma out of an M turned on its side.

MOUΣIKH-IATPEIA;

O R,

A FIDDLE the beſt DOCTOR.

New faces: Hazard, Gye and Salmon, c.1770-1774

The printing trade grew strongly in the later eighteenth century in line with a surging consumerist economy, higher levels of literacy, and a widespread public appetite for news, information, and entertainment. Nowhere was this more evident than at prosperous Bath where the number of active printers doubled between 1770 and 1774, with three more contenders joining the established trio of Keene, Martin and Cruttwell. All the parvenus were in their twenties. Samuel Hazard, a former pupil at Bath Bluecoats School, had originally been apprenticed to a local heel-maker but at some point switched to printing and was sufficiently competent by c.1770 to set up his own press in Cheap Street. He scored an early success with a minor classic of black authorship, *A Narrative of the most Remarkable Particulars in the Life of... an African Prince* by Ukawsaw Gronniosaw (alias James Albert), a c.50-page pamphlet that needed to be reprinted at least five times in the 1770s before the publication passed to William Gye. A Moravian by faith, Hazard accepted work of any religious or secular complexion – from a libretto of Handel's *Messiah* and a hymn book for the Countess of Huntingdon's chapels [Fig.28 opposite] to a string of medical publications, six by Marmaduke Berdoe and two by Daniel Lysons, on gout, optics, fevers, and other subjects, all dating from 1771-3. Printing the hymn book brought Hazard into contact with the bookseller Thomas Mills, clerk to the Huntingdon Chapel at Bath; and when Mills removed to Bristol in December 1773 Hazard took over his shop and complete stock-in-trade in Kingsmead Square and added the sale of books and stationery to his printing business.

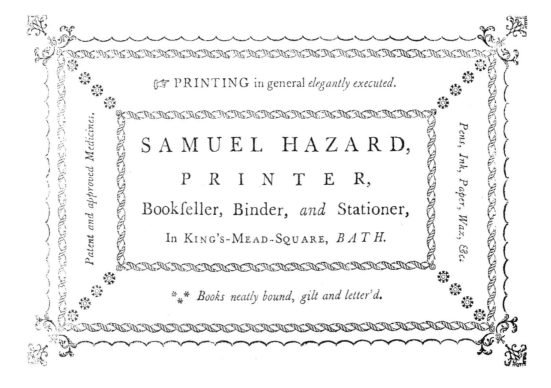

Meanwhile by 1771 the second of the three newcomers, William Gye, had installed himself in Westgate Street, financed by a legacy from his apothecary father. He conceivably learned his craft working on the *Bath Journal* under John Hooper, a family relation who in 1774 stood witness when Gye married. A specimen of his early work can be seen opposite [Fig.29], a page from a self-justifying pamphlet by the controversial preacher Henry Peckwell to the churchwarden of Winterbourne Gunner, near Salisbury, after an intemperate sermon had given offence. Gye himself risked giving offence to fellow printers by teaming up in 1773 with the third newcomer, John Salmon, to produce a newspaper, the *Bath Courant*. Too adventurous perhaps, or just undersubscribed, the paper folded after five months' endeavour. This failure seems to have cured Gye of gambles with newspapers, but Salmon, as we shall see, would try again. Hazard, by contrast, never even took the risk.

284 H Y M N CLXXXVI.

Prone to wander, Lord, I feel it;
  Prone to leave the God I love;
Here's my heart, Oh take and seal it,
  Seal it from thy courts above.

CLXXXVI. *Chrift crucified.* **L. M.**

WHEN I furvey the wond'rous crofs
  On which the Prince of Glory died,
My richeft gain I count but lofs,
  And pour contempt on all my pride.

Forbid it, Lord, that I fhould boaft,
  Save in the death of Chrift my God:
All the vain things that charm me moft,
  I facrifice them to his blood.

See from his head, his hands and feet,
  Sorrow and love flow mingled down!
Did e'er fuch love and forrow meet,
  Or thorns compofe fo rich a crown?

H Y M N CLXXXVII. 285

Were the whole realm of nature mine,
  That were a prefent far too fmall;
Love fo amazing, fo divine,
  Demands my foul, my life, my all!

CLXXXVII. *Chrift's Humiliation.* **C. M.**

WHAT objeċt's this that meets my eyes
  From out Jerufalem's gate;
Which fills my mind with fuch furprize,
  As wonders to create?

Who can it be that groans beneath
  A pond'rous crofs of wood;
Whofe foul's o'erwhelm'd in pains of death,
  And body's bath'd in blood?

Is this the Man, can this be he,
  The Prophets have foretold,
Should with tranfgreffors number'd be,
  And for their crimes be fold?

Fig.28

[3]

A

L E T T E R, *&c.*

S I R,

YOUR *Complaints* give me pain; becaufe they add to the Sorrow of poor Mrs. Coleman, whofe family affliċtion is fuch as the leaft Senfibility cannot but fympathize with.—Your *threats*, as they refpeċt none but myfelf, make lefs impreffion. My Study is, " to fhew myfelf a Workman approved of God." I cannot temporize, or trim to the Fafhion of the Times, and Tempers of Men, leaft I fhould ceafe to be " the Servant of Chrift." That *awful Day of Judgment* upon which I fpoke is at Hand, or in the Language of the Text " the " Judge ftandeth before the Door." He, the Searcher of Hearts, will decide whether I am wrong in preaching, or you in taking offence at his Word. To HIM I appeal. In that day you will be called upon to juftify your Conduċt.— Then too, I muft give an account.—Here the matter fhould have refted, but that I am inform- ed the *principal Men* of the Parifh have fuch In- fluence as may prejudice or injure the poor of my Flock. For their Sakes therefore I think it my duty to undertake the painful tafk of juftifying *the*

A 2   *Sermon*

Fig.29

THE

PRIEST DISSECTED:

A POEM,

Addreſſed to the Rev. Mr. ———,

AUTHOR OF

REGULUS, TOBY, CÆSAR,

And other SATIRICAL PIECES in the public Papers.

Calm and ſerene amid the ſcorching Flame
The Hero tug'd——and out the Monſter came.   Page 26.

BATH: Printed by S. HAZARD;

And ſold by DODSLEY, *Pall-Mall,* and WILKIE, St. *Paul's Church-Yard,* LONDON;
FLETCHER and HODSON, at CAMBRIDGE; and by FREDERICK, TENNENT,
and HAZARD, at BATH. ———

M.DCC.LXXIV.

Fig.30

Samuel Hazard and Christopher Anstey

In taking over Mills' bookshop Hazard was at pains to remind customers that he continued to print 'with elegance and dispatch', but at the same time he entered fully into his new tradesman's role. His sale catalogue in 1777 listed almost 1500 volumes, probably a mix of new and second-hand, and an interest in the antiquarian side is suggested by a later sale of notable old Bibles in fine bindings. As part of the normal bookseller's job he accepted binding commissions and was also prepared to refurbish private libraries. In 1775 he enlarged his stock of stationery with a large range of writing, printing and wrapping papers. These he sold for cash, i.e. not on credit, 'at Bristol prices', offering in return to buy supplies of clean rags for selling on to paper manufacturers. He bottled and sold his own black writing ink, and produced ruled account books to any specification. And like any bookseller he sold various brands of proprietary medicines.

During the seven or so years he spent in Kingsmead Square, Hazard's best customer for his printing services was the satirical poet Christopher Anstey, already nationally famous for *The New Bath Guide* (1766 and often reprinted) – which was no town guide at all but instead related the spa adventures of the fictitious Blunderhead family in witty, parody verse. Having subsequently settled at Bath, Anstey found himself attending Anna Miller's rather pretentious, fortnightly literary salon at Batheaston Villa, and when the coterie came under critical attack, Anstey rose to the defence with a savage rejoinder, *The Priest Dissected*, printed by Hazard in 1774 [Fig.30 opposite]. Once it emerged, however, that 'the priest' was not the anonymous critic after all, Anstey hurriedly removed copies from circulation or at least those still with the Bath, Cambridge and London booksellers named on the title-page. It was an embarrassment, but the Anstey-Hazard collaboration survived nonetheless, and besides a brief *Epistle to Mrs M*ll*r* (1776) it produced three other publications related to Anstey's latest exercise in social satire, *An Election Ball*.

Inspired by Sir John Sebright's celebratory ball on re-election as a city M.P., Anstey penned an amusing poetic skit on the event, written 'in Zomerzetshire Dialect', which he got Hazard to print off in 500 copies. The edition sold out at once, with a charitable shilling per copy from the profits going to relieve the debtors in Bath gaol. Anstey promptly enlisted Hazard to issue an expanded, re-set, second edition, this time in plain English. It reached the bookshops in March 1776 still without its intended Matthew Darly frontispiece because of 'an unfortunate accident to the copperplate'. Already, though, Anstey had asked C.W.Bampfylde, an amateur artist friend (and brother-in-law of the aforementioned Sebright M.P.) to draw a set of illustrations, to be engraved by Bath's William Hibbert, for a third edition in the autumn, but again the plates were not ready in time. In December they were eventually printed, along with a letter in Latin verse - *Epistola Poetica Familiaris*, addressed to Bampfylde in person [Fig.31 below and Fig.32 overleaf], but Bampfylde found much at fault with Hibbert's lacklustre interpretations – despite Anstey's assurances that they were liked at Bath and that William Hoare, the fashionable spa portrait painter, had himself advised Hibbert over them. In the end it was not until 1786 and the 5th edition of *The Election Ball* that the full set of six illustrations appeared.

Fig.31

Ad C. W. BAMPFYLDE, Arm:

EPISTOLA POETICA FAMILIARIS,

IN QUA CONTINENTUR

Tabulæ quinque ab eo excogitatæ,

QUÆ PERSONAS REPRÆSENTANT

POEMATIS CUJUSDAM ANGLICANI,

CUI TITULUS

An ELECTION BALL.

Auctore C. A N S T E Y, Arm:

BATHONIÆ:

Impensis Auctoris excudebat S. HAZARD:

Proftant venales apud S. HAZARD, & W. HIBBART, et fingulos ibidem Biblio-
polas. J. DODSLEY, J. WILKIE, *Londini.* FLETCHER & HODSON, *Cantab.* &
J. FLETCHER, *Oxon.*

M.DCC.LXXVI.

Pret: 5s.

Fig.32

John Salmon, 1773-1781

After splitting from William Gye in September 1773, John Salmon moved into the house and shop in Stall Street where his father Tobias Salmon, a linen draper, lived. There he set up a press and advertised that he printed handbills at short notice and books at London prices. Among examples from 1774-5 were an account of Louis XVI's coronation, a reprint of the Bath City Charter edited by Tobias Salmon, and an anthology of Latin verse composed by English authors to which Hazard, not Salmon, added a third volume two years later [Fig.33]. In 1776 Salmon entered into a brief printing partnership with Thomas Whitford, but it was his own decision to print a libellous pamphlet that September attacking John Jefferys, Bath's Town Clerk. It was true the Salmon family had a long-standing grudge against Jefferys and had targeted him before, but this time Jefferys chose to sue and indeed won his case. Convicted of malicious libel by the King's Bench, Salmon spent the summer of 1777 in a London gaol with ample time to plan the weekly print he would launch on his release.

When *Salmon's Mercury* appeared on 1 November at a mere penny a copy, its hybrid format was all about evading newspaper duty. Superficially resembling a newspaper and set out in three columns with the usual advertisements, it contained no official news. Moreover, since it was printed not on the single sheet of a typical newspaper but on a sheet-and-a-half, it could claim to be a pamphlet and so pay only three shillings tax per edition instead of a penny per copy – a strange pamphlet, nonetheless, with totally renewed content every Saturday. The subterfuge was too transparent to last and *Salmon's Mercury* soon became a more orthodox, 4-page, two-penny weekly with a heavy emphasis on entertainment. In its second year of publication much space was given over to Salmon's detailed case against Jefferys, which must surely have alienated some readers and reduced revenue from advertisements. From November 1779 Salmon altered the *Mercury's* lay-out to two columns set in larger type, and somehow kept it going for at least another eighteen months until 11 May 1781, date of the last known issue.

SELECTA

POEMATA

ANGLORUM

LATINA,

SEU SPARSIM EDITA,

SEU HACTENUS INEDITA,

ACCURANTE

EDVARDO POPHAM,

Coll. Oriel. OXON, *nuper Soc.*

Multa Poetarum veniat manus.　　HOR. Sat. 4.

VOL. II.

BATHONIÆ
EXCUDEBAT J. SALMON.
Proſtant venales apud W. BALLY *ibidem Bibli-opolam.* J. DODSLEY, et W. GOLDSMITH *Londini.* FLETCHER & HODSON *Cantab.* J FLETCHER *Oxon.*
1774.

SELECTA

POEMATA

ANGLORUM

LATINA;

SEU SPARSIM EDITA,

SEU HACTENUS INEDITA;

ACCURANTE

EDVARDO POPHAM,

Coll. Oriel. OXON. *nuper Soc.*

Extremam hanc oro veniam. —　　VIRG.

VOL. III.

BATHONIÆ
Excudebat S. HAZARD:
Proſtant venales apud M. BALLY, *ibidem Bibliopolam;* J. DODSLEY, & G. GOLDSMITH, *Londini;* FLETCHER & HODSON, *Cantab.* & J. FLETCHER, *Oxon.*
M.DCC.LXXVI.

Fig.33

Cruttwell's progress, 1775-1779

For domestic and foreign news one turned not to *Salmon's Mercury* but to the *Bath Journal* or the *Bath Chronicle*, which both now freely reported parliamentary proceedings. Around 1770, like many other newspapers, they had taken a stand on freedom of the press, had even given tacit approval to the libertarian John Wilkes and referred to Commons and Lords debates in defiance of the ban. By 1772 that battle had been won. Tongue-in-cheek allusions to Parliament as 'a certain political club' or 'the Robin Hood Society' were no longer necessary; controversial matters like the rights of American colonists or the conduct of the war could henceforth be reported at will. Neither the *Journal* nor the *Chronicle* took an overtly party line, yet by news selection and presentation (and by printing readers' letters) they still influenced opinion, especially on critical issues. Anti-government feeling over Admiral Keppel's trial in 1779 – to take just one example – was undoubtedly fanned by their vivid press reports as well as by a series of pamphlets that Cruttwell produced detailing the entire trial and the national celebrations that followed Keppel's acquittal.

Back in St James's Street after a three year interlude at 11 Union Passage (1772-5), Cruttwell was busier than ever. Besides the weekly *Chronicle* and an unknown quantity of handbills, cards, tickets, warrants and official forms, he printed far more pamphlets and books than any of his competitors, and by 1776 he was advertising for a clerk to keep track of all the accounts. The same year he ventured into magazine publishing in association with London and Bristol booksellers and his own brother at Sherborne. Despite the new set of Caslon type supplied from Birmingham and a specially commissioned William Hibbert frontispiece, the *Bath and Bristol Magazine* survived for only two or three volumes. The handsome Caslon type was displayed to good effect, though, in other Cruttwell imprints of the time, as in the younger John Wood's brief text accompanying the plates to *The Description of the Hot-Bath at Bath*, printed by Cruttwell in 1777 [see detail below, Fig.34].

twenty-four hours, a circumſtance that proves how well the water is ſecured by the cylinder, for in Dr. Guidot's time, about the year one thouſand ſix hundred and eighty-one, by the water's riſing through rubbiſh and looſe earth, the ſpring produced for the uſe of the community only one hundred and eight tons and a quarter in the twenty-four hours; and from that time to the year one thouſand ſeven hundred and ſeventy-three, when the bath was pulled down, the quantity of water decreaſed to eighty-four tons in the twenty-four hours; ſo that we now have water in the proportion of five to three, more than in the year one thouſand ſeven hundred and ſeventy-three; and in the proportion of nearly four to three more than in Dr. Guidot's time.

Fig.34

Freeman of the Stationers' Company, Cruttwell had a reputation for elegant printing. He was also a respected public figure – proprietor of the *Chronicle*, churchwarden of St James's, freemason, founding member in 1777 of the prestigious Bath and West of England Society, a sociable man whose web of contacts decidedly served his business interests. His friendship with the Bath and West's secretary, Edmund Rack, proved especially fruitful. Besides executing work for Rack in person (*Mentor's Letters*, 1777; an edition of Jacob Duché's *Caspipina's Letters*, 1777; *Essays, Lectures and Poems*, 1781), Cruttwell found himself unofficial printer to the Bath and West well into the future, printing its successive *Rules and Orders* and, from 1780 onwards, the Society's widely influential series of *Letters and Papers on Agriculture, Planting, &c.* This was the target audience too for *A General Dictionary of Husbandry, Planting, Gardening...* issued in a two-volume set in 1779.

Cruttwell likewise tapped into the coteries of Lady Miller at Batheaston and the historian Catharine Macaulay in Alfred Street. For the former he printed all four 'Batheaston Vase' anthologies, *Poetical Amusements at a Villa near Bath* (1775-81), each volume being sponsored by a different Bath bookseller (Bull, Frederick, Tucker, Pratt & Clinch) and the profits all going to charity. The Catharine Macaulay connection went back to 1774-5 when Cruttwell printed two of her pamphlets, and then in 1777 the flattering *Six Odes presented to... Mrs Catharine Macaulay*. More importantly, in 1778 she entrusted him with the continuation of her 8-volume *History of England*, though only the first of two intended volumes ever appeared. Further jobs came Cruttwell's way through two particular Macaulay admirers, the irrepressible quack doctor James Graham and the Rev.Thomas Wilson. Several of Graham's amusingly outrageous works bear Cruttwell's name, including the 4th edition of *The General State of Medical and Chirurgical Practice* of 1778. Wilson's significance came later, as we shall see, through his wish to see the works of his late father, the Bishop of Sodor and Man, decently published.

Even bread-and-butter tasks were neatly dispatched – as with this partial list of lodgings (including two at bookshops) from *The Stranger's Assistant and Guide to Bath* for 1777.

MILSOM-STREET.

Mrs. Dart	Mrs. Elliot
Mrs. Pyne	Mr. Strawbridge
Mr. Coe, 2 houſes	Mr. Bacon, 2 houſes
Mr. Gordon, 2 houſes	Mrs. Garlick
Mr. Bally, bookſeller	Mr. Tennent, bookſeller
Mrs. Langhorn	Mr. Shaw
Mr. Ewing, brewer	Miſs Plura, millener
Mr. Crofs, upholder	Mrs. Walters
Mr. Madden	Mrs. Leary
Mrs. Prynn	Mrs. Stephens

GREEN-STREET.

Miſs Robe, mantua-maker

What is striking about any list of imprints from later Georgian Bath is the diversity. In the three years 1777-9, when Cruttwell produced on average at least a book a month, we find Robert Hitchcock's comedy *The Coquette* jostling for attention, among much else, with a medley of turnpike statutes, midwifery advice, cotillion dance steps, precepts on agriculture, odes, essays, sermons (one of them by Joseph Priestley, then living at Calne), and not least the first volume of Ann Thicknesse's *Sketches of the Lives... of the Ladies of France*. But while Cruttwell's list was eclectic, its detectable literary bias presumably reflected his own taste, witness the care he took over the *Bath and Bristol Magazine* and the occasional miscellanies he gave away with the *Bath Chronicle* from January 1772.

EPITAPH *on* Dr. DODD.

HERE fleeps, inurn'd, the minifter to woe,
That taught the heart to feel—the eye to flow;
From whom diftrefs ne'er came with bofom griev'd,
Whofe tongue perfuaded, and whofe hand reliev'd;
What eye, unbloated, could obferve his fall?—
Juft—where he could—benevolent to all.
Here ceafe enquiry—bleffing made him bleft;
Let pity veil the Page that fpeaks the reft.

Fig.35

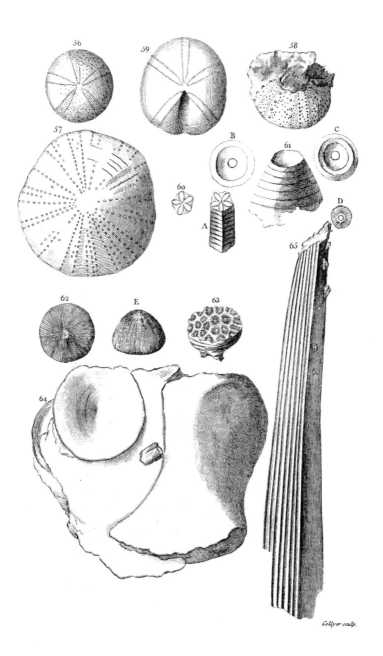

Fig.36

Hooper & Keene, Gye, Hazard, 1776-1780

Bath's oldest printer, John Keene, died in February 1777 after almost twenty-one years as proprietor of the *Bath Journal*. The firm passed jointly to his son Thomas Keene and to John Hooper who had managed the newspaper operation during John Keene's tenure. Next to files of the *Journal* little has survived of their production other than theatre playbills (a long-time Keene specialty) and the odd trade-card – mere remnants, no doubt, of a myriad small printing jobs they carried out.

Little remains either from the press of William Gye at this period beyond playbills, notices, a handful of pamphlets, and a single book – the 300-page reprint of Elisha Cole's seventeenth-century Calvinist homily *A Practical Discourse of God's Sovereignty* (1776). The latter, with a preface by the Huntingdonian pastor William Romaine, had advance orders for almost a thousand copies, including fifty for Samuel Hazard and a hundred for the London bookseller J.Matthews who both had a financial stake in the publication. Such reprints were now legitimate following a recent House of Lords ruling that the notion of perpetual copyright claimed by some bookseller/publishers had no basis in law.

A pamphlet that Gye published in July 1777, *A Narrative of the late William Dodd* [detail, Fig.35 opposite], capitalised on the intense local interest in the Rev. Dr Dodd, a former royal chaplain and a preacher at Bath's Margaret Chapel, who had just been hanged for forgery. Gye must have been touched by the story of the contrite Dodd sermonising to his fellow inmates in Newgate gaol, and by the vain public petitioning for his reprieve. The lot of prisoners nearer home would soon be concerning him greatly as he took up the cause of the many small debtors languishing in Somerset gaols.

If Cruttwell enjoyed the lion's share of book printing at Bath, Hazard never ceased to be a worthy contender. His collaboration with Anstey in the 1770s has already been mentioned, but he worked as well with other local authors such as the satirist Joseph Draper and the naturalist John Walcott whose monograph on the Jurassic fossils of the Bath neighbourhood, *Descriptions and Figures of Petrifactions,* is illustrated opposite by one of the sixteen full-page plates [Fig.36]. Next to these more-or-less luxurious publications should be placed the dozens of tracts and sheets, mainly but not wholly religious, that Hazard printed in large editions for the wider market. Some sample titles, all available by 1779, will sufficiently convey the flavour.

> Joseph Belcher, *The Life of Faith*
> *Character of the Right Hon. the Countess of Huntingdon*
> *Devout Thoughts of the Retired Penitent*
> *Divine Admonitions*
> *The Experience and Happy Death of Sarah Long*
> *Furniture for the Mind, or the Best Gift to Servants*
> Richard Hill, *Several Seats in Parliament to be had Gratis*
> *A Hymn to the God of Abraham*
> *A Journey from Time to Eternity*
> *A Letter from a Religious Friend under Spiritual Trouble*
> *Parable of a Pilgrim*
> *Reform or Ruin abridged*
> *The Supreme Good: a Poem*
> *Three Dialogues between a Minister and one of his Parishioners*

Priced at a penny or two pence a copy, these would be sold not only from Hazard's own bookshop (with discounts for orders of multiple-copies) but also no doubt through street hawkers and country dealers who obtained supplies directly from Hazard on credit. From October 1780, though, they had to seek him out at a new address, no longer in Kingsmead Street but back in busy Cheap Street where his career began. Here almost at once he opened a circulating library, extending it in 1784 by a comfortable upstairs reading room well stocked with newspapers and magazines. But he still sold books and stationery; he still took on binding work; and his printing press remained as active as ever.

The printing office

A basic jobbing printer could doubtless work from a single room with hardly more assistance than family members and an apprentice boy to 'devil' for him at the press. Bath's larger printing houses had a more elaborate set-up, and though no detailed office plans, inventories of equipment, or lists of staff have come down to us, a good deal is known or can be inferred about the city's various printing establishments. They were, for instance, sited centrally, not in the growing suburbs. Most would be fronted at street level by a retail shop, very likely accompanied by a window display showing samples of printing, stationery and branded medicines to catch the attention of passers-by. Retailing was a necessary part of the business, and besides vending their own wares provincial printers served as agents for nationally advertised products – from London-printed books and magazines to cough cures and lottery tickets. The retail shop would also take in copy for printing jobs (including advertisements and news items in the case of Bath's newspapers) and handle customers' subscriptions, bills and payments. Samuel Hazard's shop on the south side of Cheap Street was extensive enough to house a circulating library with a first-floor newspaper reading room. In late 1791, after the widening of Cheap Street (a disruptive event that had obliged Hazard to vacate his premises for months), his library amounted to over 10,000 volumes. The printing side of his business was probably carried on, quite separately from the genteel library, in a property he part-tenanted on the north side of Cheap Street. William Meyler adopted a similar solution in the 1790s when he added printing operations to his well-established bookshop and library in Orange Grove, keeping his presses out of the way of other business in Kingston Building nearby.

Whether working from separate buildings, back rooms, or basements, the larger printers needed adequate floor space, with as much daylight as possible (to save on candles), a source of water (for dampening the paper before printing, and washing down type afterwards), and high racks for drying newly printed sheets (with the help, when necessary, of fires or stoves). Storage had to be found too for bales of paper, for cases and baskets of heavy loose type, for galleys and packets of standing type, and for the printed or half-printed sheets as they accumulated. The compositor(s), pressmen, and warehouse man (and any bookbinders there might be in-house), all occupied their own distinct but connecting spaces. Only the corrector and his reading boy could easily work on a different floor.

A small printing shop could manage with capital of £300 according to a sale notice in 1810, but that figure must be considerably scaled up for larger establishments. Indeed a substantial London printing office of the period, furnished with nine presses and nearly 30,000 lbs (pounds) of type, was worth £2000-£3000, up to ten times as much. Standard printing presses were not themselves a great expense however. A brand-new press could be had for £20-£30, and a good secondhand one for £12-£15, as Bath advertisements show. What evidence there is suggests that a medium-size provincial printer would typically own a couple of printing presses, though a simple 'Job Office' (as witness a small business advertised at Bath in 1804) might operate with only one. A larger enterprise like Cruttwell's, printing a weekly newspaper as well as quantities of books, pamphlets, and jobbing work, could easily have kept three or more presses regularly on the go, with one of them perhaps dedicated to quick jobs and pulling proofs. Some printers also had binders' presses. A printing office advertised in 1800, for example, contained an iron-screw standing press and two cutting presses. Around 1797 Hazard may even have owned some kind of calendering machine since he was certainly experimenting at this stage with a hot-pressing technique to give his printed sheets a glazed finish. Almost certainly he and Cruttwell possessed their own cylinder rolling presses for intaglio work (as Thomas Boddely had around the middle of the century). The alternative would have been to rely on specialist engravers to provide sets of copperplate illustrations all ready printed for binding up.

Easily the heaviest capital cost was the purchase of type, either new or second-hand. Any printing office capable of pamphlet work and small books needed an array of different-size roman and italic founts, including at least a bill or so of Brevier (point 8), Long Primer (point 10), Pica (point 12, equivalent to the default fount on a modern computer), English (point 14), and Great Primer (point 18), together with some larger letter for handbill display, and with rules, ornaments, and a few woodcut devices besides. Even that would not satisfy all demands. John Salmon, for instance, in May 1779 lacked the symbols (apart from simple numerals) to print mathematical problems in *Salmon's Mercury*, and Richard Cruttwell still had no Greek alphabets in 1774 when he wanted them, though he did soon acquire Greek and eventually Hebrew characters and Black Letter (Gothic) as well.

By the 1780s printers of Cruttwell's and Hazard's stature could offer founts from as small as Pearl (point 4) up to Double Pica (point 22) and beyond. Cruttwell himself habitually used Caslon typefaces, whereas Hazard favoured the products of the Bristol-London type-founders, Joseph & Edmund Fry, from whom he also obtained his stocks of ornamental 'printers flowers'. Illustrated below at enlarged size are fairly restrained, early examples of Hazard's floral typography from Daniel Lysons' *Practical Essays upon Intermitting Fevers* (1772). Some of his later creations in this genre were admired for their almost pyrotechnical exuberance.

Printers commonly ended up with an assortment of type acquired at different periods – an increasing tendency in the decades around 1800 as transitional and modern faces began to supersede older designs. They would nevertheless be reluctant to jettison their older stocks overnight. Book printing consumed quite large quantities of type, especially if it involved setting long texts or required type to be kept standing in galley for reprints and new editions. Even a relatively slim 100-page octavo set in Pica would take the bulk of sixteen pairs of cases (800-1000 lbs) of type to compose. This put constraints on the volume of work that could be processed at any one time and encouraged the printing of books in stages, so that type could be distributed back to the cases as soon as proofs had been corrected and enough sheets for each gathering had been worked off at the press.

Presses and stocks of type represented capital assets, but publication costs themselves depended mainly on the current price of consumables (30-50% of the total) and labour (20-35%). Paper – generally of linen or cotton rag – was by far the most expensive single item, and for this reason printers tended to hold minimal permanent stocks, buying in fresh batches for each major job and using up imperfect or spoiled sheets for proofing and wrapping. Bath printers were probably supplied from mills and paper warehouses around London or from Bristol, though a paper-mill existed at Twerton c.1727-80, with others later on at Combe Down (i.e. De Montalt mill from 1805, making high-grade writing and artists' papers) and at Bathford (from 1810). By 1790 smoother, Baskerville-style 'wove' paper began very slowly to replace traditional laid paper (with its prominent chain-lines) for printing books. Occasionally tinted paper was employed, or extra-fine paper for special copies of a edition and for high-quality engravings. As regards ink, local printers turned for the most part to specialist manufacturers outside Bath – Cruttwell in 1798 even sold a parchment ink made in York and could easily have obtained barrels of printing ink from the same source. Hazard on the other hand prepared his own, at least in the 1770s, though blending and refining the linseed oil and lampblack to the right consistency must always have been a messy business.

Procedures

Every publication, even a simple handbill, began as a text. This would normally be in the form of an author's manuscript or, in the case of a new edition, of a printed original marked up with revisions. Before printing could get under way there were practical matters to be settled – intended format, paper size, type body, print-run, special features such as footnotes or illustrations, style of issue (in sheets, stitched, in paper covers or boards), as well as questions of financing, publicity, distribution, and likely selling price – all decisions that might also involve bookseller third-parties who were sharing the risks and expectations of publication. The standard book and pamphlet formats were duodecimo and octavo, printed respectively at 24 or 16 pages per sheet on Crown or Post paper (roughly 50 x 38cm). The more luxurious quarto or folio formats, sometimes using larger sheets of Demy and Royal, were reserved most often for poetry, history, and other elevated material, though ordinary handbills and public notices were necessarily printed in these formats too – or bigger still for special display items like Charles Mayo's *A Compendious View of the History... of Europe... 1755-89*, a tabular display poster created by Hazard in 1789 on sheets of Atlas (76 x 66cm) wove. Print-runs were generally calculated in multiples of 250 copies, but any number could be run off in practice – from the large editions of 'Cheap Repository Tracts' that Hazard turned out in 1795-6 down to the mere twenty-five copies of *A Journal of the Shrievalty of Richard Hoare, Esquire*, a prestige quarto printed by Cruttwell in 1815.

As soon as format and print-run were agreed, an estimate could be made of how many sheets would be required, an easier task when working from a fair copy than from an ill-written manuscript full of blots and revisions. Paper could then be set aside or ordered, the work scheduled, the job entered in the press book, and the compositor eventually set to work. Like the pressmen the compositor was employed on piece rates, though he was paid better than they were on account of his special expertise. Setting copy demanded concentration and judgment as well as mechanical skill. Even if the author's text had already been prepared by the printer's corrector, the compositor still had to edit it for house style, punctuation, use of upper case and the like, while at the same time assembling and spacing the lines of type at a rate of maybe a thousand sorts (letters, points, etc.) an hour, and adding pagination, headings, catchwords, signatures, and footnotes as necessary. A liberal education was almost expected of compositors at Bath's leading printers, required as they sometimes were to set quite erudite texts or passages in Latin and Greek. At least Greek typography was no longer plagued with all the ligatured letters and contractions it once had been, and Hazard's compositor follows the modern simplified style in this example from Demetrius de la Croix's *Connubia Florum* printed in 1791.

Plin. Nat. Hiſt. Lib. xvii. 37. Ed. Harduin.

Tom. iii. 404. 405.

Τάχα δὲ καὶ γένει τινὶ δένδρων ἔνια κατὰ φύσιν αὐτομάτως
τε γινόμενα, καὶ ἐ κακᾶμενης ἀλλ' εὐθενᾶσης οἷον τῆς
ϖεύκης, ὅταν αἱ ῥίζαι δαδωθῶσι. πάσχᾶσι μὲν γὰρ τᾶτο
δι' εὐϊροφίαν καὶ δι' ὑϖερβολήν. ἅμα δὲ τῇ δαδώσει τὴν τρο-
φὴν ᾶ διεῖσαι φθείρονlαι. καὶ ἔοικε ϖαραϖλήσιον τὸ συμβαῖ-
νον τῷ ἐϖὶ τῶν ζώων, ὅταν ὑϖερϖαχυνθῶσιν. ᾶ δυνάμενα
γὰρ ἕλκειν τὴν πνοὴν, ᾶ δ'ὅλως τῷ ϖνεύμαlι χρῆσθαι, διὰ
τὴν σύμφραξιν καὶ τήν πύκνωσιν· ἐκεῖνά τε ἀποϖνίγονlαι,
καὶ αἱ ϖεῦκαι.

Imposition – i.e. filling the forme with the pages of set type in their correct order and orientation – was the compositor's responsibility, before the pressmen briefly took over and pulled a first 'revise' proof. This went to the corrector for proofreading, a task sometimes aided by an apprentice boy reading aloud from the author's script in a singsong voice as the corrector checked the printed sheet.

Correcting the type itself was more laborious work, since the compositor, using a bodkin and leaning over the forme, now had to find, extract, and replace each wrong sort and, if need be, re-space the lines. Once this was done, however, a further proof could be taken and then saved until the whole set of proofs was ready for the author or corrector to make a final check. Alternatively, to prevent the type waiting around in formes, each proof sheet could be checked as it appeared and the whole run of that sheet printed off before the next was even imposed. This plainly happened with the enlarged second edition of *Sonnets, chiefly written at Picturesque Spots*, printed by Cruttwell in 1789 for the well-known clerical poet, W.L.Bowles. Here a note on p.31 in gathering H calls for the reader to insert a word on p. 27 in gathering G - clear evidence that the volume was being checked and printed off sheet by sheet and not all at one go. That method of pointing out residual errors was rare. The usual solution was to issue a list of errata among the 'preliminaries' (title-page, contents, etc) – the section of the book printed last. The apologetic list below [Fig.37] comes from William Matthews, *The Miscellaneous Companions* (Cruttwell, 1786) and suggests that all three volumes had gone though the press before the mistakes were detected.

E R R A T A.

EVERY one who has any knowledge of printing, is apprized of the difficulty there muſt be, in getting even three ſuch volumes as theſe wrought off, without ſome errors. But the candid reader will obligingly make allowances for ſuch as have occurred in this work, and correct with his pen, as follows; or any other error which may have been overlooked.

VOLUME I.

Page 22, line 13, for *any more than*, read *as well as.*
77, l. 8, f. *bis*, r. *their.*
78, l. 22, f. *eaſt*, r. *north-eaſt.*
120, l. 6, f. *poet's*, r. *poetick.*

VOLUME II.

Page 122, l. 24, after *creation*, inſtead of *ends*, inſert a ſemi-colon.
160, l. 3, f. *the*, r. *though.*
174, l. 14, f. *following*, r. *this.*
226, l. 3, f. *him*, r. *God.*

VOLUME III.

Page 44, l. 2 of note, dele comma after *is.*
45, l. 3, f. *a God*, r. *God.*
99, l. 13, dele *ſeriouſly.*
162, l. 16, at the end, dele comma, and inſert *was.*
170, l. 1, after *complete*, inſert THEOPHILUS.
192, l. 2, f. *moſt*, r. *more.*
197, l. 17, inſert a ſemicolon after *regions*, and the comma at *bear.*
ib. l. 22, f. *thyſelf*, r. *thou art.*
209, l. 16, f. *alone*, r. *only.*

Fig.37

Seeing their manuscripts translated into the objective medium of print opened authors' eyes. In the introduction to his *Poems on Various Subjects* (Boddely, 1754) Samuel Bowden admitted that, while some faults were down to having the book 'printed in the country', he was equally conscious of 'many blunders and puerilitys' of his own as soon as they were in cold type. A later author pleaded illness while his book was in the press for a whole page of errata. Another blamed his lack of leisure or 'inclination' to revise his initial manuscript. A third, perceiving a lack of clarity in his newly printed words, added a last-minute appendix with extra information. William Tickell, by contrast, shrugged off the minor blemishes remaining in *A Concise Account of... Anodyne Aetherial Spirit*, printed by John Salmon in 1787 – 'The intelligent reader will meet with several typographical errors, but as they will obviously appear to him as such, they have been left to stand uncorrected'.

If the original composed type had been retained, a near reprint could be produced with minimal effort on the part of the compositor beyond correcting errata, updating the title-page, and imposing the formes for the press. Revisions to the original text, on the other hand, caused him much more trouble, because even a single substantial change often had repercussions on many succeeding pages of type. Such modifications can followed illuminatingly through successive editions of the Bath guidebooks. Cruttwell's *New Bath Guide* (biennial 1770-6, then annual) underwent constant evolution over the years as information was updated from edition to edition, wording modified, new material inserted, and the odd engraving or decoration replaced. Wherever possible, serious disruption of the existing lay-out was avoided by making adjustments elsewhere. The 1796 edition of the guide, for example, added a fresh section on the recently opened Private Baths, and then by way of compensation abbreviated some of the earlier text on the spa's bathing establishments. Even so, with this and other changes, the complete contents filled an extra page and forced the printer to move details of the Bath postal services onto the inside of the back cover. Cruttwell may well have kept a working copy of the latest *New Bath Guide* at the ready in order to note down revisions for the next edition. This was William Meyler's policy in the early nineteenth century with the *Original Bath Guide*, and indeed he displayed interleaved versions, updated by hand, at his circulating library for subscribers to consult.

Whether the task was a new book, a reprint, or a revised edition, it made no difference to the pressmen since these all demanded equal effort. Working the press was a strenuous physical occupation – 'beating' the imposed type with inkballs, securing the sheets on the tympan, rolling the carriage into position, pulling twice on the platen, removing and storing the still dampened sheets – the whole cycle of operations being repeated every thirty seconds or so. No wonder that an advertisement for a pressman's apprentice in 1808 specifies 'a stout lad' and that Cruttwell expected his pressmen to be sober and diligent. After manning the presses they would wash the formes of type in a trough of lye, rinse them clean, and leave them to dry, before returning them to the compositor either for storing away or, more usually, for distributing into the cases again, with care not to create 'pie', i.e. any muddle of letter and fount. A small establishment would have no warehouseman, so it probably fell to the pressmen to look after the supplies of paper, to dampen the sheets for printing, and to dry and store them afterwards.

Maintaining a regular workflow must have depended on teamwork, especially in a firm like Richard Cruttwell's which liked to guarantee its regular journeymen 'constant employment' and never took on casual labour or 'travelling printers'. In 1793 his main establishment, including Cruttwell himself and his eighteen-year-old son, amounted to only eight men – judging, that is, from the names listed in the Bath Loyal Association's record book, which many local printers signed as proof they had no seditious leanings. This total would exclude apprentices, however, and it should be remembered that an older, experienced apprentice could almost stand in for an actual journeyman. Indeed in 1793 one of Cruttwell's former apprentices, George Steart, had just completed his term and was sufficiently well trained to launch out at once as an independent Bath stationer/printer. The statistic of eight staff takes no account either of other family members, especially women, who may have fulfilled a vital economic role in the firm – serving in the retail shop for example. In comparison, and at this same date, the printer William Gye seems to have employed four journeymen besides himself and his son. The workforce of the other leading printers at Bath must have been comparable.

How duties were spread among Cruttwell's team is debatable. The elder Cruttwell presumably managed the business, appointed staff, negotiated terms with authors, booksellers and joint publishers, and decided the weekly content of the *Bath Chronicle*. The younger Cruttwell, already being groomed to take over the firm, quite likely learned to set type, and either he or his father could easily have acted as corrector of proofs without employing a special man. Assuming a ratio of two compositors to three pressmen, the sixth employee, given the scale of business and the newspaper side, was possibly a clerk responsible for correspondence and accounts – a post Cruttwell had once advertised in fact. But that leaves no room for the presence of a bookbinder on the site.

In 1778 Cruttwell gave up binding and sold off his tools to a local bookseller. That surely meant only that he stopped 'finishing' books in vellum or leather to special order, for most of them still had to be 'forwarded' (the first stages of binding), and Cruttwell went on issuing them ready sewn, in blue covers or in boards, as well as in the option of unbound sheets. All the folding and pressing, cutting and sewing, and attaching of boards must still have taken place in the printing office, and it was only a matter of time before Cruttwell was again advertising for a bookbinder competent in 'different branches' of his craft. By 1806 that covered both 'elegant' and 'plain' work, which suggests a range of bindings - simple millboard, vellum, calf, morocco, etc., with tooling and gilt as necessary, but perhaps not the silk, satin, and velvet finishes that ornamental bookbinders could offer. Bath was well endowed with bookbinders by the 1780s, some working freelance, others for the printers and booksellers, and when a local binder disposed of his tools and presses in 1784 he assured potential buyers they could expect ample custom. No Bath printer yet issued trade bindings, but coloured and printed paper covers were in common use, sometimes to create a distinctive uniform look. Take Cruttwell's annual moneyspinner, *The House-keeper's Accompt* [or *Account-*] *Book*, always presented as a Demy-size quarto in blue covers, which became a familiar sight in many households after its first appearance in late 1772. It was also one of the rare Bath publications of the period to be partly printed in coloured ink, when – from 1793 onwards – the horizontal rules across each weekly page were added in red, a novel extra task for the pressmen.

Before a book could be bound, it had to be collated, i.e. assembled in its correct sequence guided by the unique alphabetical signature assigned to each gathering. It was at this point that any separately printed illustrations were inserted. The print shown below [Fig.38] was added as a voguish frontispiece to Sir Edward Harington's 'dramatic fable' *The Sheep, the Duck and the Cock* (Cruttwell, 1783) concerning a flight at Versailles in the early days of the ballooning craze. Placing a frontispiece like this was simple. Finding the sites for plates within the body of the book took a little more trouble.

Fig.38

Publishing Bishop Wilson

The work that most established Cruttwell's national reputation for fine printing was the Bishop Wilson *Bible* of 1785. On his death in 1755 the pious Thomas Wilson, Lord Bishop of Sodor and Man for nearly sixty years, had left a mass of mostly unpublished writings to his son, Rev.Thomas Wilson. In the 1770s the latter's house in Alfred Street, Bath, hosted the cultish literary circle associated with Catharine Macaulay, through whom he perhaps first met Richard Cruttwell and his elder brother Clement. This was the catalyst for publishing the Wilson manuscripts, because Clement Cruttwell, though still a practising surgeon, was preparing for the Anglican priesthood and would make an ideal editor.

In late 1779 the proposals to print the Bishop's *Works* were duly announced and a two-guinea subscription list opened. A year later the two handsome Royal quarto volumes of tracts and sermons were ready on time, printed from specially purchased new Caslon type and delivered to subscribers in boards for their personal choice of binding. On the very heels of this first edition, Cruttwell advertised a second subscription in order to exploit further his valuable array of standing type – not a 2-volume set this time but a reissue in 84 sixpenny numbers in a larger folio format. This finally came out between November 1781 and October 1782 – produced towards the end at a rate of three numbers per week, each containing three sheets (twelve folio pages) of letterpress. Both editions were soon available in bound form as well, the 2-volume quarto version clad luxuriously in morocco or turkey at £5 15s. 6d., the other as a single volume covered more cheaply in calf at £2 12s 6d.

But this was not the end of it. An 8-volume octavo edition in boards appeared in late 1783, with the popular volumes 5-8, containing just the sermons, on separate offer. Cruttwell brought out further octavo reprints in 1791 and 1796, and also issued excerpts as publications in their own right, e.g. *Principles and Duties of Christianity* reprinted in 1789 for Sunday schools, and *Thirty-three Sermons* in two duodecimo volumes, 1791, done at the behest of the SPCK. Among other individual titles *The Sacra Privata, or Private Mediations* is worth particular notice for its nineteenth-century devotional significance to Anglo-Catholics. Yet Wilson's ecumenical piety appealed at the time to all denominations, and the undoubted success of the *Works* must have encouraged Cruttwell as he embarked on the prestigious venture of the Wilson *Bible*.

In theory only the university presses of Oxford and Cambridge enjoyed the legal right to print English-language Bibles, but this privilege could easily be circumvented by commentated versions – which in effect the Wilson *Bible* was. Once again edited by Clement Cruttwell, it reproduced the 1611 authorised text entire, but added all the variants from other English translations plus Bishop Wilson's own detailed notes from his manuscripts. Everything was done to make the publication special. The subscription proposals announced in June 1783 promised a work in three volumes quarto, printed from specially cast Caslon type on Royal Woodbaston vellum paper, with all the profits going to an appropriate charity supporting the families of deceased Manx and other local clergy. Four leading London publishers shared the copyright, but over the next two years and more the Cruttwell brothers carried all the responsibility for organising and supervising the production, which on top of all else demanded unusually meticulous proofreading. It called indeed for a long-sustained effort on the part of a provincial printing house which was at the same time busy with other commissions, not to speak of turning out a weekly newspaper. In the end, occupying nearly three thousand pages of print, the Wilson *Bible* appeared in October 1785 and was quickly hailed as a masterpiece of elegant printing, a judgment that may be confirmed from the sample shown opposite [Fig.39]. Subscribers received their copies, issued simply in boards, for a reasonable three guineas while non-subscribers paid 50% more. Ten fine copies were exceptionally printed on wider-margined large paper.

Such scrupulous care was not lavished on every item that passed through the Cruttwell presses – witness the broken and uneven line-ruling observable in the table partly reproduced opposite as Fig.40 (from William Brooke's *Plans of the Sunday Schools...,* printed in 1789). Although the standard of Cruttwell's output was seldom less than competent, a distinction was clearly made between routine (and no doubt cheaper) jobs and the more prestigious commissions entrusted to his most skilful and experienced workmen.

I. PETER V.

Anno Domini 60. in the faith, [x] knowing that the fame afflictions are accomplished in your brethren that are in the world.

A prayer. But the God of all grace, [y] who hath called us into his eternal glory by 10 Chrift Jefus, after that ye have fuffered [z] a while, [a] make you perfect, [b] ftablifh, ftrengthen, fettle *you.* [c] To him *be* glory and dominion for ever 11 and ever. Amen.

Conclufion. [d] By Silvanus, a faithful brother unto you, as I fuppofe, I have [e] written 12 briefly, exhorting, and teftifying [f] that this is the true grace of God wherein ye ftand. The *church that is* at Babylon, elected together with *you,* faluteth 13 you; and *fo doth* [g] Marcus my fon. [h] Greet ye one another with a kifs of 14 charity. [i] Peace *be* with you all that are in Chrift Jefus. Amen.

[x] Acts 14. 22. 1 Theff. 3. 3. 2 Tim. 3. 12. Chap. 2. 21.——[y] 1 Cor. 1. 9. 1 Tim. 6. 12.——[z] 2 Cor. 4. 17. Chap. 1. 6.——[a] Heb. 13. 21. Jude 24.——[b] 2 Theff. 2. 17; 3. 3.——[c] Chap. 4. 11. Rev. 1. 6.——[d] 2 Cor. 1. 19.——[e] Heb. 13. 22.——[f] Acts 20. 24. 1 Cor. 15. 1. 2 Pet. 1. 12.——[g] Acts 12. 12, 25.——[h] Rom. 16. 16. 1 Cor. 16. 20. 2 Cor. 13. 12. 1 Theff. 5. 26.——[i] Ephef. 6. 23.

in the faith—by faith. *Ham.* in faith. *Pu.* *the fame afflictions &c.*—your brethren in the world have even the fame afflictions. *Co.* you do but fulfil the fame afflictions which are appointed to your brethren. *Ma.* the fame afflictions befal your brotherhood, which is in the world. *Ham.* the fame fufferings to be accomplifhed on your brotherhood &c. *Pu.*
accomplifhed in—appointed unto. *Cr.* made to. *Rb.*
10. *us*—you. *Wb.* *a while*—a little affliction. *Bi.* a little. *Gen. Rb.* *make you perfect*—fhall his ownfelf make you perfect. *Co. Ma. Cr.* himfelf reftore you, or, fhall himfelf reftore you. *Ham.* will make you perfect. *Wb.* compleat you himfelf. *Pu.* *ftablifh, ftrengthen, fettle you*—fhall fet-

tle, ftrengthen, and ftablifh you. *Co. Ma.* fettle, ftrengthen, ftablifh you. *Cr. Bi.* confirm, ftrengthen, and ftablifh you. *Gen.* confirm and ftablifh you. *Rb.* eftablifh, enable, fix. *Pu.*
11. *glory and*—omitted, *Wb.* dominion—might. *Pu.*
12. *briefly*—by reafon of a few things. *Pu.* exhorting—befeeching. *Wi. Rb.*
13. The companions of your election, which are at Babylon, falute you, &c. *Co. Ma.* the church—fhe. *Wb. Pu.* *elected together with you*—your fellow-chofen. *Ham.* chofen together. *Pu.*
14. *kifs of charity*—holy kifs. *Wi. Rb.* kifs of love. *Co. Ma. Cr. Gen. Pu.* *Jefus*—omitted, *Wb. We.* *Amen*—omitted, *Wb. We.* fo let it be. *Pu.*

Accomplifhed in your brethren. i. e. Undergone by all other Chriftians in thefe days of perfecution.
10. *Perfect*—in patience.——*Settle you*—in the faith.
12. By Sylvanus, whom I believe to be a faithful honeft man, by him I have written &c.
The true grace of God. The only doctrine by which you can be faved.
13. *At Babylon:* viz. At Rome; or, as Bp. PEARSON, *(Oper. pofthum.)* from Babylon in Egypt, which is the moft likely opinion.
14. *All that are in Chrift Jefus.* All that profefs Chriftianity.

Fig.39

Mrs.   WEEKLY SCHOOL,   1788.

	1	2	3	4	5	6	7	8	9	10	11	12	13	14	15	16	17	18	19	20	21	22	23	24	25	26	27	28	29	30	31
1 A.B.	./.																														
2 A.C.	2/.																														
3 A.D.	6/.																														
4 A.E.	./2																														
5 A.F.	./3																														
6 A.G.	3/4																														
7 A.H.	6/.																														
8 A.I.	./5																														
9 A.K.	./6																														
10 A.L.	1/.																														
11 A.M.	./7																														
12 A.N.	1/1																														

EXPLANATION.

1 Prefent Morning and Afternoon.
2 Abfent at Morning Roll-Calling.
3 Abfent all the Morning.
4 Abfent at Afternoon Roll-Calling.
5 Abfent all the Afternoon.
6 Abfent Morning and Afternoon.
7 Sick in the Morning.
8 Sick in the Afternoon.
9 Sick Morning and Afternoon.
10 Abfent with leave in the Morning.
11 Abfent with leave in the Afternoon.
12 Abfent with leave both Morning and Afternoon.

The Number of Sick, abfent with or without Leave, being deducted from the Total effective Number, fhews the Number prefent each Day.

Fig.40

Imprints, 1781-1790

Throughout the 1780s the names of Richard Cruttwell and Samuel Hazard continued to predominate on books and pamphlets printed at Bath, though as in earlier decades a proportion of authentic Bath imprints carried no printer's name at all and cannot always be assigned to a particular firm. The Hooper & Keene partnership meanwhile concentrated mainly on jobbing work together with the weekly task of producing the *Bath Journal*. William Gye, still printing from 4 Westgate Buildings, was increasingly preoccupied with other concerns. Stirred by the hopeless plight of small debtors held in local prisons, especially at the remote county gaol of Ilchester, Gye took up their cause in earnest, visiting prisoners himself and constantly raising funds for their release or at least to supply provisions and fuel. Early in 1787 he arranged a debtors' benefit concert at the Guildhall, having already printed large quantities of his pamphlet *The Test of Philanthropy, Charity and Benevolence*, which was not priced but invited donations. All this made him widely known across Somerset and perhaps incidentally brought in work – e.g. printing the libretto for Handel's *Messiah* performed at Wells in 1788.

The tone of Hazard's output was equally serious. Nearly 70% of the titles he printed in this decade were religious in character, ranging from single sermons to substantial books, and covering different Christian positions from High Church (e.g. Charles Daubeny's *Twelve Lectures on the Church Catechism*, 1788) to Moravian, Hazard's own persuasion. The other 30% or so divided sharply into the didactic and the entertaining. In one category a Latin tutor (*Grammaticae Quaestiones*, 1783) by the headmaster of Bath Grammar School, Nathanael Morgan; a technical artist's treatise on oil painting (*An Essay on the Mechanic of Oil Colours*, 1787); and a 1200-page historical reference book in six duodecimo volumes (*The Historical Pocket Library, or Biographical Vade Mecum*, 1790, Fig.44). In the other category a 4-volume domestic novel, *Agnes De-Courci*, by an established circulating-library author, Agnes Maria Bennett, and several books of verse – among which the first Bath edition of Christopher Anstey's *Liberality or Memoirs of a Decayed Macaroni* (1788), a fine 16-page quarto containing an apt new illustration [Fig.41]:

Fig.41

The engraver's art had by now been extended by the tonal technique of aquatint. Rarely employed in Bath publications, the method was nevertheless tried out in Philip Thicknesse's pamphlet describing his Lansdown house, *A Sketch of St Catherine's Hermitage*, printed by Cruttwell in 1787 [Fig.42 opposite]. Was it perhaps the work of William Gingell, an engraver just established at Bath?

S.t CATHERINE'S HERMITAGE. near BATH,

Fig.42

Cruttwell was altogether more prolific than Hazard. The sheer variety of his book printing at this period is apparent even in a brief sampling of titles.

A Second Collection containing the Figures of 25 Favourite Cotillons (1781)
William Falconer, *An Account of the Epidemic Catarrhal Fever... called Influenza... at Bath...* (1782)
Simeon Moreau, *A Tour to Cheltenham Spa* (1783)
F.Soule, *A New Grammar of the French Language* (1783)
Abstracts... of Acts of Parliament passed in the Session of 1784 (1784)
Edward Davies, *Aphtharte, the Genius of Britain: a Poem... in the Taste of the Sixteenth Century* (1784)
Thoughts on East-India Affairs... By a quondam Servant of the Company (1784)
J.M.Adair, *Medical Cautions for the Consideration of Invalids* (1785)
Albinia Gwynn, *The History of the Hon.Edward Mortimer. By a Lady* (1785)
J.Z.Holwell, *Dissertations on the Origin, Nature and Pursuits of Intelligent Beings...* (1786)
F.X.Vispré, *A Dissertation on the Growth of Wine in England...* (1786)
The Heetopades of Vishnu-Sarma. Translated by Sir Charles Wilkins (1787)
A Scheme to pay off... the National Debt by a Repeal of the Marriage Act (1787)
Chipping Sodbury Friendly Society, *Rules and Orders* (1788)
W.L.Bowles, *Fourteen Sonnets... written during a Tour* (1788)
James Graham, *A New, Plain and Rational Treatise on... the Bath Waters* (1789)
Cornelius de Pauw, *Selections from 'Les Recherches Philosophiques sur les Américains'.* Edited by
    D.Webb (1789)
Clement Cruttwell, *Concordance of Parallels from Bibles and Commentaries... in Hebrew, Latin,
    French, Italian, Spanish, English, and other Languages* (1790)
Hints for the Management of Hot-Beds and... Culture of Early Cucumbers... (1790)

Metropolitan connections

More often than not the names of London bookseller/publishers appeared on the title-pages of books printed at Bath unless their content was purely local. The reasons were economic. Notwithstanding the dramatic spread of book production outside the capital, London remained the great literary marketplace, the heart of the domestic book trade. To secure one or more London partners in advance of any provincial publication was a guarantee of extra promotion and sales, and might even dictate whether publication went ahead in the first place. Borzacchini's Italian grammar [illustrated opposite, Fig.43] offers a typical enough example of shared distribution. Here the author, a successful language master at Bath, presumably initiated publication and paid Cruttwell to print his text on the strength of an advance agreement with two named London booksellers (as well as three at Bath, including Cruttwell himself) to advertise and sell the book. The same method had been adopted two years previously for Borzacchini's companion French grammar, *The Parisian Master*, only with a slightly different mix of London and Bath booksellers plus two others at Bristol

Business deals might be tailored to a book's likely readership. A new edition of Theocritus and other Greek authors, translated by Richard Polwhele and printed by Cruttwell in 1792, naturally had the support of Oxford and Cambridge booksellers. John Feltham's *A Tour through the Island of Mann* [Isle of Man], another Cruttwell imprint (1798), listed sponsoring booksellers in Liverpool and Whitehaven where good sales could be expected. Books of regional interest or by locally known authors commonly name booksellers in Bristol, Exeter, Salisbury and other places.

But London booksellers were far and away the most important associates of Bath printers. Some thirty different firms struck deals with Cruttwell and Hazard in the two decades 1781-1800, either on their own or alongside other booksellers. Half-a-dozen of these names crop up quite often in Bath imprints, and above all Charles Dilly (bookseller at 22 Poultry, and publisher of Boswell's life of Samuel Johnson), who appears, for example, on both the Borzacchini publications mentioned above. Other prominent collaborators at this period included James Dodsley, the dissenting publisher Joseph Johnson, Vernor & Hood, John/F.& C.Rivington (publishers to the SPCK), and the large wholesaler G.G.& J.Robinson. Often the London bookseller acted simply as a retailing and publicity agent, holding stock of particular titles and entering them in his catalogue. But joint publication with copyright shared between Bath and London was also not unknown, as when Cruttwell and Dilly joined forces in publishing an anonymous two-volume romantic novel, *The Count de Santerre*, in 1797.

Collaboration might take a more active form. By the late eighteenth century the reputation of Cruttwell and Hazard for reliable work at competitive rates was such that copyright-holding London booksellers would sometimes send books to Bath for printing despite the additional transport costs involved. The publication shown opposite [Fig.44] is a case in point, a 6-volume set printed by Hazard for a Ludgate Street stationer. Three years later Hazard printed an admirable large quarto, *A Critical Inquiry into... Alexander the Great*, on behalf of G.G. & J.Robinson, the Paternoster Row bookseller. This required the setting of French, Latin and Greek text yet produced commendably few errata – among them the odd direction 'for Volga read Wolga passim'. A more straightforward commission in 1795 set Hazard on a reprint of Salomon Gessner's *The Death of Abel* in Mary Collier's thirty-year-old translation – the copyright having meanwhile passed from Dodsley to Vernor & Hood who provided Hazard with new engravings to bind in with the printed text.

One further example of the practice of 'putting out' printing jobs to Bath concerns the well-regarded local author, Richard Graves, rector and private schoolmaster of Claverton. Graves had always had his novels and other works published and printed in London through the bookseller Dodsley, but in 1792 Dodsley declined Graves's Greek translation, *The Meditations of Marcus Aurelius*, saying it was 'not the sort of reading suited to the present age'. Graves took it to another London publisher, G.G.& J.Robinson instead, probably with the recommendation that Cruttwell, whose expertise he knew, should print it. The collaboration worked and was repeated in 1793 with Graves's next book, *The Reveries of Solitude*. Cruttwell went on to print all Graves's later publications, including a volume of sermons in 1799.

THE
TUSCAN MASTER;

OR A

NEW AND EASY METHOD

OF

ACQUIRING A PERFECT KNOWLEDGE

OF THE

ITALIAN LANGUAGE

IN A SHORT TIME,

DIVIDED INTO TWO PARTS:

CONTAINING

THE RUDIMENTS AND THE SYNTAX
OF THE LANGUAGE;

COMPOSED, DIGESTED, AND EXPLAINED,

IN A MORE CONCISE, ACCURATE, AND EASY MANNER
THAN ANY EVER YET ATTEMPTED.

By Dr. M. GUELFI BORZACCHINI,

Profeffor of the Italian and French Languages.

Bath

PRINTED AND SOLD BY R. CRUTTWELL, FOR THE AUTHOR;
SOLD ALSO
BY S. HAZARD, AND L. BULL, IN BATH;
AND C. DILLY, POULTRY, AND J. BOFFE, GERRARD-STREET,
SOHO, LONDON.

Fig.43

Publifh'd May 1ft 1789 by G. Riley, Ludgate Street.

THE
HISTORICAL
POCKET LIBRARY;
OR,

BIOGRAPHICAL VADE-MECUM.
SIX VOLUMES.

CONSISTING OF

I. The HEATHEN MYTHOLOGY.
II. ANCIENT HISTORY.
III. The ROMAN HISTORY.
IV. The HISTORY of ENGLAND.
V. GEOGRAPHY.
VI. NATURAL HISTORY.

THE WHOLE FORMING A

MORAL and COMPREHENSIVE SYSTEM

OF

HISTORICAL INFORMATION,

FOR THE

Amufement and Inftruction of the young Nobility
of both Sexes.

BATH: PRINTED BY S. HAZARD;
FOR G. RILEY, STATIONER, LUDGATE-STREET,
LONDON.——1790.

Fig.44

Bath's own publisher/booksellers

Ever since Thomas Boddely's day, Bath printers had published occasional pamphlets and books on their own initiative. Nothing strange in that, but local booksellers who were not printers themselves also ventured into publishing, just like their London counterparts albeit on a much smaller scale. Henry Hammond had established the tradition as early as 1697, and his successors Samuel Leake and William Frederick had more than kept it up, undertaking dozens of books over the years, sometimes acting together and often in association with particular London and provincial booksellers.

Other booksellers followed suit. William Taylor, who had learned his trade under the famous Leake before opening a quite independent shop and circulating library in 1762, adopted the *New Bath Guide* soon afterwards (printed first by Cornelius Pope, then by Cruttwell) and issued it through many editions down to 1795 when, on his death, his daughter Ann took on the profitable responsibility. It was a task of constant revision, not least in the frequent touching up of William Hibbert's frontispiece map [illustrated here from the 1790 edition, Fig.45] to take account of the relentless urban expansion. Taylor also published Bath maps in individual sheets – jointly from c.1783 with a colleague bookseller, William Meyler.

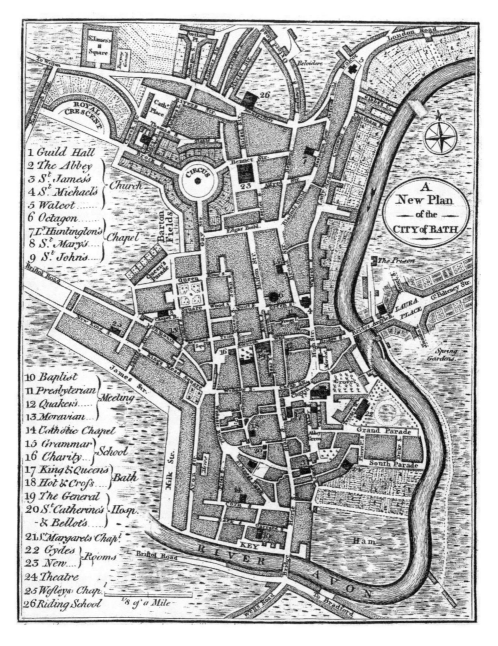

Fig.45

Local maps, guidebooks, and directories, being assured of a ready sale, proved irresistible subjects for other would-be publishers. The stationer John Basnett brought out a city map in 1770, as did the Milsom Street booksellers, Bally & Tennent, a year later. The latter map was a sufficiently valuable property to be acquired and republished by another bookselling partnership, Pratt & Clinch/Pratt & Marshall. And besides these there were maps showing the larger Bath region, some of them available in hand-coloured versions. The Bath engravers William Hibbert and William Gingell could both reproduce an uncomplicated map or plan, but for high-class cartography Charles Harcourt Masters turned to a specialist London engraver, S.I.Neele, in his beautiful survey maps of Bath published from 1789 onwards.

The long-sustained Taylor/Cruttwell series of Bath guidebooks was, by contrast, hardly challenged until 1801-11 when the printer/bookseller John Browne came out with four successive editions of his *Historic and Local New Bath Guide*. This encouraged rival products from competitors – John Savage and William Meyler's *Original New Bath Guide* (1804 onwards) and Wood & Cunningham's *Improved Bath Guide* (1811-1816). Directories of residents and tradesmen were more onerous to compile. The first reasonably comprehensive work of this kind appeared under the name of another printer/bookseller, George Robbins, as late as 1800, followed by John Browne's versions in 1805 and 1809, and Wood & Cunningham's later on.

Such publications doubtless sold well and created a welcome buzz of publicity around their producers, but they are less intriguing than some of the other titles that booksellers staked their judgment and money on. Spa literature was of course a fairly safe bet. Tennent in 1772, Taylor in 1774 and 1785, and Meyler in 1795, all published studies by different authors on the Bath or Cheltenham waters. Several religious items printed for the nonconformist bookseller Thomas Mills in 1768-73 had a clear sectarian audience in view, while T.Shrimpton's *Remarks* [by a Marine Officer] *on the... Trial of the Hon.Augustus Keppel*, issued in numbered parts in 1779, was simply a nonce publication taking advantage of the national excitement over the court-martialing of a naval hero. Books of verse, however, must have been a riskier proposition, though several Bath booksellers did publish them. Another bookseller, John Campbell (of Campbell & Gainsborough), published two works of his own, *Pious Records* – which attracted nearly four hundred subscribers in 1791 – and then in 1793 the highly topical *Predictions of the Singular Events in France.* Pratt & Clinch did something similar with the 3rd edition of Samuel Jackson Pratt's novel *Emma Corbett* in 1781, but then Pratt was an established author (writing under the pseudonym Courtney Melmoth), in demand at all the circulating libraries and not just his own at the top of Milsom Street. Indeed the copy of *Emma Corbett* in Bath Central Library still bears the labels of Bally's library in the same street, and the novel is prominently listed by its title in Samuel Hazard's self-printed library catalogue of the same period [detail below].

178   *N O V E L S,* &c.

5476 Eugenia and Adelaide, 2 vols. 5s. 6d.
5477 Euphemia, by Mrs. Charlotte Lennox, 4 vols. 12s.
5478 Exceſſive fenſibility, 2 vols. 6s.
5479 Emily Montague (hiſtory of) in letters, 4 vols. 10s.
5480 Emma Corbett, 3 vols. 7s. 6d.
5481 Evelina—or the hiſtory of a young lady's entrance in-
      to the world, by Miſs Burney, 3 vols. 9s.
5482 Explanation—or agreeable ſurpriſe, 2 vols. 5s. 6d.
5483 Emilius and Sophia, from the French of Rouſſeau, 4
      vols.
5484 Errors of nature, 3 vols. 8s. 6d.
5485 Errors of innocence, 5 vols. 15s.
5486 Emmeline, 3s.
5487 Excurſion, 2 vols. 6s.
5488 Eden Vale, 2 vols. 6s.
5489 Eugenius, 2 vols. 6s.

Collinson's *Somerset*

Publishing by subscription was a practical, if time-consuming, means of financing certain publications, especially books with a hint of exclusivity about them destined more for private libraries than for common use. Usually a down payment of around 50% of the intended price was expected on subscribing, in return for which the subscriber was issued with a receipt to produce when the book was ready and the rest of the payment became due. Various inducements would be offered – an advantageous price, the printing of subscribers' names in the finished book, perhaps copies signed by the author, and normally a guarantee that the work would proceed once a stated minimum number of copies had been spoken for.

Dozens of Bath books owed their existence to the subscription method. Sarah Fielding's *Xenophon* and the Bishop Wilson *Bible* have already been mentioned, and others included William Renwick's novel *The Unfortunate Lovers* (1771), the younger John Wood's *A Series of Plans for Cottages* (1780), Edmund Rack's *Essays, Letters and Poems* (1781), and an annotated edition of the four Gospels by Pasquier Quesnel (1790). Ann Thicknesse's *Sketches of the Lives and Writings of the Ladies of France* (1778-81) would simply not have been viable without subscribers – or at least not the second and third volumes, for the first volume, not published by subscription, had made no profit whatsoever, and only a subscription started by friends induced her to complete the set.

One of the key books of the period – John Collinson's long-gestated county history of Somerset – depended wholly on advance subscriptions. As usual the undertaking began as a set of proposals. Broadcast in the regional press in September 1784, these were sent out as well to potential private subscribers accompanied in some cases by a further personal letter of appeal and by sample printed entries for two localities, Chilcompton and Porlock. The printer Cruttwell, already intimate with Collinson's chief collaborator, Edmund Rack, was therefore involved from the start and probably advised on the 3-volume quarto format and the three-guinea subscription price. Topographical plates were to embellish the work, and here the choice of draughtsman engraver fell not on the familiar Hibbert or Gingell but on Thomas Bonnor who since 1782 had been making a name for landscape prints and views of Bath.

Over the next few years, as the number of subscribed copies surpassed a safe five hundred mark, the labour of research, writing and illustrating went on despite Rack's untimely death in February 1787. A few months later the publication was reported to be 'well advanced', with seventeen of Bonnor's plates already viewable in proof to encourage other estate owners to sponsor engravings of their own country seats. It remained a leisurely process all the same and subscribers had to wait another five years until their patience was rewarded. Although Cruttwell had finished printing the entire text of some 1500 pages early in 1792, the last plate proofs (either Bonnor's or the frontispiece map by A.Crocker of Frome dated March 1792) were run off only in August, and *The History and Antiquities of the County of Somerset* finally delivered in December. From the initial announcement to eventual publication it had taken over nine years and by now some subscribers seemed reluctant to pay the residual charge and collect their sets. Some may even have lapsed, since as late as February 1797 a handful were still being urged to pick up their copies or else forfeit their down payment. A few sets of the *History* were then still available for non-subscribers at £4 14s. 6d. – 50% more than the original subscription price but a bargain nonetheless considering the steep inflation at this period. The man behind the whole project, John Collinson, had died at an early age in 1793 within nine months of publication, his last months not helped by sour reviews of his great endeavour in the *Gentleman's Magazine*. Cruttwell's reputation, on the other hand, can only have been enhanced by yet another demonstration of classic printing [Fig.46 opposite]. He also contributed materially to the success of the work by ordering fifty advance copies to sell, at a profit of course, in his own shop.

Some subscription proposals came to nothing. Confidently announced, they fell by the wayside for lack of public support, though at least after testing the ground. Others took time to build a full list. Even the subscription for Richard Warner's indispensable *The History of Bath* stayed open for three and-a-half years before the volume finally appeared at the start of 1801. Cruttwell, as so often with subscription books, was again the printer, but Hazard too occasionally worked on titles published this way, as with *Annals of Virtue* by the notorious Mme de Genlis which he printed in 1794.

𝕭𝖆𝖙𝖍-𝖋𝖔𝖗𝖚𝖒.]   WIDCOMBE and LYNCOMBE.   169

That part of the parifh which ftill retains the name of Lyncombe is nearly half a mile to the fouth of the laft-mentioned ftreet, and is fituated in a deep, winding, and romantick valley, watered by a fmall ftream, and interfperfed with gardens, meads, and woods.   In this retired fpot are four modern-built elegant houfes; one of which is called the Spa, from a mineral fpring difcovered here in the year 1737, which was for fome time much frequented by thofe afflicted with the ftone and gravel, and other diforders; but it has been long fince difufed.   At about a furlong eaftward is another fpring of the chalybeate kind, in the garden of a houfe called the Bagatelle formerly a publick tea-houfe.   On the flope of the hill (which rifes, cloathed in wood, on the weft fide of Lyncombe) is a houfe of publick entertainment, much reforted to by parties from Bath, called King James's Palace, from a tradition that he concealed himfelf in this retirement feveral months after his abdication of the Crown. A quarter of a mile hence towards the eaft ftands a group of five neat houfes) four of them newly erected) on an eminence, denominated, from its fituation on the ridge of the hill, Hanging-Lands, and commanding a fine profpect of Bath, and the circumjacent country.

Immediately over Holloway, and part of Claverton-ftreet, hangs Beechen-Cliff, cloathed half way down its precipitous flope with fine coppice wood.   This hill rifes upwards of three hundred and fixty feet above the Avon, and affords from its fummit a fingular bird's-eye view of the whole city, the vale ftretching to Bath-Ford on one fide, and to Kelwefton on the other, with the Avon winding through it, and the ranges of the furrounding hills.   On the north fide of this fteep, a little above the upper part of Holloway, are remarkably fine fprings and refervoirs, which fupply by pipes the lower part of the city of Bath with water; for which an acknowledgment is paid by the corporation to the hofpital of Brewton.

But what moft attracts obfervation in this parifh, is the ftately manfion of Prior-Park.[*]   This magnificent building ftands on a terrace about one hundred feet below the fummit of Combe-down, and four hundred feet above the city of Bath, from which it is a mile and a half diftant to the foutheaft.   It confifts of a houfe in the centre, two pavilions, and two wings of offices, all united by arcades, and making one continued line of building, between twelve and thirteen hundred feet in front, of which the houfe occupies one hundred and fifty.   It is built in the Corinthian ftile upon a ruftick bafement, and crowned with a balluftrade.   The centre part, projecting from the plane, forms one of the moft correct and noble porticoes in the kingdom, fupported by fix large, lofty, and fuperb columns.   The apartments are very fpacious, elegant, and warm, free from damp, and healthy.   At the bottom of

[*] So called from its being built on lands formerly belonging to the Priors of Bath, who had a grange near the fpot, and a park well ftocked with deer.   Leland takes notice of this park; but he tells us that in his time it had no deer, and that the inclofures were become ruinous.   " A mile a this fyde *Bathe* by Southe Eft," fays he, " I faw 2 Parks enclofyd withe a ruinus Stone Waulle now withe out Dere.   One longyd to the Bysfhope, an othar to the Prior of *Bathe*."   Itin. vol. vii. p. 100.   After the diffolution thefe lands were granted to Humphry Colles, who fold them to Matthew Colthurft.   MS. Donat. in Muf. Brit.

Fig.46

THE BATH HERALD; & GENERAL ADVERTISER.

COUNTRY NEWS.

GLOUCESTER, FEB. 28.

A bag-fox was lately turned out before the Gloucester hounds, which, after a chace of 30 miles without a check, was killed near Winchcomb. The fox took a course through some of the deepest parts of the vale, which had exhausted the horses extremely, before they came to the hills above Cheltenham, so that three persons only were in at the death; and we hear, that the severe running has proved fatal to two of the horses of considerable value.

Several of the country papers speak of the benefits and success of the House of Industry.—One of the best and most profitable parochial institutions in this neighbourhood, we believe, is at Ledbury, where the poor, that a few years ago were a heavy expence, now produce by their labour an annual profit.

HANTS.—Lately died at Fordinbridge, Mary Watts, a poor old woman, whose lethargic habit of body had for three years been very extraordinary, and had lately so considerably increased, that she would sleep a week, a fortnight, and, sometimes a month, or more, at a time, which she considered but as a day. Her son, a weaver, with whom she lived, was accustomed to watch her very attentively, and his usual method of waking her from her torpor, was by putting food into her mouth. When awake, she would partake of a small aliment, chiefly liquid, and quickly fall into the same state again. Many efforts were often in vain made to rouse her. She awoke about three hours before her death, and continued awake, apparently in good health and spirits, till the moment of her dissolution.

HEREFORD, FEB. 25. A very remarkable match, between two famous runners, for 100l. a side, was determined near this city. The one was a Welshman, from Ross, in this county, and the other a native of Staffordshire. The distance was ten miles, viz. from the first to the sixth mile stone, on the Hay road, and back.

The Welshman gained the bet with apparent ease, performing the journey in one hour and six minutes: his antagonist lost by about 400 yards, and nearly four minutes in point of time.

IPSWICH, FEB. 25. Friday evening the 24th inst. between seven and eight o'clock, the following disasterous circumstance happened at the Salt-office, Woodbridge: As George Hall, one of the men employed there, was skimming a pan of boiling liquor, he unfortunately fell in and was scalded most shock-

GRISKIN CLUB.

"TO THE EDITOR OF THE BATH HERALD.

SIR,

I HAVE been for some time engaged in collecting materials for a "History of the Clubs of Great-Britain," of which the metropolis has furnished an ample portion. I am now visiting the cities and principal towns of the provinces, to enquire after such Societies as are distinguished by particular institutes, and local peculiarities: There is one of this kind, I

ed to ; which will ensure a valuable wheat crop the succeeding year. The feed saved by this method of planting beans is very considerable, as instead of three or four bushels, three or four pecks are fully sufficient for an acre, the intervals between the rows being three feet and seven inches between each bean in the rows. Nor need the trembling farmer fear if his ground be in tolerable tilth, that his crop will be diminished by this small quantity of seed, as the superior tillage will amply compensate for it by many single beans throwing out three or four stalks, from the ample room given their roots to search for food. If the ground be remarkably strong, the three feet intervals may be extended to four feet, lest the luxuriance of the beans should interrupt and overshadow the growth of the cabbages. Cabbages raised from seed the preceding August, and transplanted into a warm spot before the winter, where they may be enabled to resist its rigour, and planted out in May, are found to succeed better than those raised in March, and planted out at Midsummer. The objection usually made to this double cropping, from the teams not being able to come into the field without damaging the cabbages, is easily remedied by the farmers neglecting to plant with cabbages those spots from the gate where he introduces his waggon, to the middle of the field, or to any other part where his own sagacity points out to him it may be necessary to conduct and turn it. On these spots he may plant his beans thicker, and experimentally discover the benefits of a small quantity of feed and horse-hoing, in preference to close planting in the common way.

If the foregoing process be justly pointed out, two crops, instead of one, may be raised in the same year, from the same ground, and neither injured by its vicinity to the other ; as the cabbages will thrive better for being secured at that scorching season from the rays of the sun, and the beans promoted in their growth, by the early fallow and destruction of the weeds.

Agriculture.

...ing the season for sowing BEANS, a few ...ticed, founded on some little reading, and ...experience, may not be unacceptable to ...general, through the channel of the ...D.

...many improvements in Agriculture, ...verizing the soil, and destroying the ...obtains the first rank : But as the ...f a whole field is attended with the ...crop, this inconvenience, has, by ...Mr. Tull, been removed, by sow-...traight parallel lines, at three feet or ...ce from each other; which enables ...e-hoe the intervals as oft as his judg-...y the nature of the soil, shall deter-...rse-hoing is far from injuring the ...ontributes greatly to its increase, as ...ng the weeds, as giving the roots of ...r range to extend themselves in quest ...nefits of horse-hoing are so great, as ...ible without experience, though it ...me time confessed, that some care is ...conducting it ; as for instance, that ...heavy soils cannot be touched with ...n the other hand, if in dry weather ...o long neglected as to become very ...ded to the difficulty of breaking the

Fig.47

The birth of the *Bath Herald*

On 3 March 1792 Bath's newspaper count doubled at a stroke, as two upstarts suddenly intruded on the space inhabited, for over a decade now, solely by Cruttwell's *Chronicle* and Hooper & Keene's *Journal*. The time for upstarts seemed ripe. Bath was booming – expanding faster, doing more business, seeing more visitors than ever before, overtaking many other regional centres in population growth and commercial opportunity. One of the upstart journalists, William Meyler, made this very point, arguing that the recent increase in 'buildings and inhabitants' had made a third newspaper 'necessary'. But a more pressing argument was perhaps the growing public hunger for news, and especially foreign news. Developing events in France, fascinating and alarming at the same time, raised fears of revolution or even moderate reform at home: and at Bath too where subversive literature was known to circulate and where the first French émigrés were already seeking refuge. No wonder that Hazard was thinking of adding the *Gazette Nationale* to the thirty-odd English-language newspapers available at his circulating library. Nor that, in order to provide greater coverage of news, the *Bath Chronicle* moved over in January 1792 to printing on larger sheets, and would, two years later, add an extra column to its four-column lay-out to accommodate more print.

William Meyler, proprietor of the new *Bath Herald and General Advertiser*, needed little introduction to a local audience. Trained under the Bath bookseller Andrew Tennent, he had since 1780 run a well-patronised bookshop and circulating library of his own in Orange Grove, and a licensed national lottery office besides from 1790. Like most other booksellers he did have some experience of publishing, but embarking on a newspaper was still a major step. Was he moved to action by the arrival in Green Street of a printer with the right expertise, or did R[ichard?] Paddock, the printer in question, settle there because the job awaited him? Whatever the case, Meyler's advance publicity stirred up opposition – not from the existing newspapers but from what Meyler called 'a numerous Co-partnership' backing a rival enterprise, the *Bath Register and Western Advertiser*. This was to be printed and published by an experienced hand, J.Johnson, from premises at 16 Stall Street, and sold for a cost-cutting 3½d. instead of the now standard 4d. We cannot object, Meyler responded, the road is open to all, so let the test be which of 'the Rival Prints... shall be made the most useful and entertaining to the Public'.

Both papers declared their political impartiality, though Meyler's actual sympathies were clear enough before the end of the year when he became secretary to the Bath Loyalist Association. The outsider Johnson was more of an unknown quantity. Going out of his way in May 1792 to denounce Thomas Paine's *The Rights of Man* ('that vile libel on our HAPPY CONSTITUTION'), he found himself a few months later in republican hands when responsibility for the *Register* passed to Campbell & Gainsborough, booksellers in Burton Street. The Gainsborough of the partnership (the artist's great nephew) died soon after, however, leaving J.C.B.Campbell, an active Methodist and committed political reformer, to oversee publication until December – at which point a group of unknown shareholders took over. The changes of ownership probably reflected the newspaper's financial insecurity given the unprofitable 3½d. cover price. As losses continued to mount, a merger with Meyler's more successful *Bath Herald* was mooted and eventually achieved in September 1793 under the amalgamated title of the *Bath Herald and Register*. The deal entailed Johnson, not Paddock, printing the paper – the position until March 1794 when Paddock replaced him, a year before Johnson's death. There was just a hint that Johnson had not always been very businesslike.

Under Meyler, an occasional poet and amateur actor, the *Herald* had a certain literary character. Issued late on Friday with a Saturday date, it nevertheless printed a full quota of news from dispatches, correspondents and the London press, but always denied it sought to sway opinion –'We smile at... [the] idea of Influence' – despite boasting 'a great, increasing Circulation'. It was certainly decently printed. Fig.47 opposite, a detail of page 4 from the *Herald*'s very first issue, 3 March 1792, shows Paddock deploying a range of type from English (for the title) down to Long Primer, Bourgeois and Brevier, in both roman and italic, with one word 'Agriculture' picked out in black-letter. Note also his and Meyler's advertisements in the last column.

The Old Man, His Children, and the Bundle of Sticks.

A FABLE.

A Good old man, no matter where,
　　Whether in York or Lancaſhire,
Or on a hill or in a dale,
It cannot much concern the tale ;
Had children very much like others,
Compos'd of ſiſters and of brothers ;
In life he had not much to give,
But his example how to live ;
His luck was what his neighbours had,
For ſome were good and ſome were bad ;
When of their father death bereft 'em,
His good advice was all he left 'em.
This good old man who long had lain,
Afflicted with diſeaſe and pain ;
With difficulty drew his breath,
And felt the ſure approach of death.
He ſtill had liv'd an honeſt life,
Kind to his neighbour and his wife ;
His practice good, his faith was found,

Obedient to the good old man,
They all to try their ſtrength began ;
Now boy now girl ; now he now ſhe,
Apply'd the faggot to their knee ;
They tugg'd and ſtrain'd and try'd again,
But ſtill they tugg'd and try'd in vain ;
In vain their ſtrength and ſkill exerted,
The faggot ev'ry effort thwarted.
And when their labour vain they found,
They threw the faggot on the ground.
　Again the good old man proceeded,
To give th'inſtruction which they needed :
Untwiſt ſays he the hazel bind,
And let the faggot be disjoin'd ;
Then ſtick by ſtick, and twig by twig,
The little children and the big,
Foll'wing the words their father ſpoke,
Each ſprig and ſpray they quickly broke :
There father ! all began to cry,

Fig.48

Hazard and the 'Cheap Repository Tracts'

Bath's master printers and leading booksellers were King-and-Country loyalists almost to a man – the bookseller J.C.B Campbell, who dared to retail Thomas Paine, perhaps the solitary exception. Hazard was as staunch as any, and his name as printer appeared at the foot of the Bath Association's loyalist broadside, worded by William Meyler, in December 1792. Shocking therefore, ten months later, to discover a renegade within his own ranks – one of his journeyman printers, George Wilkinson, an avowed supporter of the republican Irish and the enemy French. Wilkinson was quickly informed on, brought to trial, fined and imprisoned, and Hazard's reputation for political soundness remained intact.

It was not just his politics, nor his serious Moravian principles, that made him an agent in Hannah More's 'Cheap Repository Tracts', a series of moral tales, improving verse, and 'Sunday reading' published in massive quantities from 1795. The redoubtable Hannah More, Evangelical campaigner, social critic, founder of the famous Mendip schools, saw the Tracts as a way of beating the purveyors of irreligious, seditious literature at their own game, swamping them by sheer numbers. She may well have been recommended to Hazard by the Bristol bookseller Thomas Mills whose former Bath shop Hazard had originally taken over – just as Mills' daughters had taken over the More sisters' former Bristol school. Alongside his more prestigious commissions, Hazard had for years been printing penny, two-penny and three-penny chapbooks and posters, mostly of a moralistic or religious nature, to sell on the streets or give away to the poor. That was exactly what Hannah More wanted, but no sooner had she approached Hazard as possible printer than her scheme was adopted and extended by her fellow Evangelicals in London and so turned into a national project. Instead of producing the 'Cheap Repository Tracts' alone, Hazard would therefore share the task with a London printer, John Marshall.

It was still a formidable job – not so much in the initial typesetting (the chapbooks rarely exceeded 24 duodecimo pages) as in the endless presswork. Hazard's team must have worked at full stretch to complete the first batches of chapbooks and broadsheets by the launch date of 3 March, the day that Bath's street hawkers, ribbons in their hats, assembled outside the Cheap Street shop to receive their stock. Copies were mostly priced at ½d. or 1d., with bulk discounts for hawkers, shopkeepers, and the many subscribers to the scheme wanting to distribute free copies. Thanks largely to these, the demand soon became insatiable. The *Bath Chronicle* reported 300,000 copies sold in the first six weeks and the presses hardly able to keep abreast of orders arriving from all parts of the country. Hazard must have dedicated at least one press full-time to the operation, yet somehow the 26 or so titles (c.17 chapbooks and 9 broadsheets) that he printed in such vast quantities through 1795, failed to stem his output of other publications. His compositors thus never lacked work. Tract publications like *The Two Shoemakers*, *Daniel in the Den of Lions*, or the broadsheet *The Old Man, his Children and the Bundle of Sticks* [detail, Fig.48 opposite] mingled in the printing office workshop with the freshly printed sheets of quite different fare – satirical verse, a French historical novel, an inquiry into cases of drowning, and, more unexpectedly, a thousand-page edition of the *Koran* in George Sale's English translation.

Within a year, however, Hazard was being phased out. Maybe his office work was to blame – Henry Thornton, the 'Cheap Repository Tracts' treasurer, considered him a good printer but a poor businessman 'mixing enthusiasm with worldly concerns'. Printing the series in two places may have become uneconomic anyway, especially after a policy decision to print henceforth on two different qualities of paper, one for hawkers, one for middle-class customers. Hazard seemingly felt disgruntled too by the preference shown to Marshall, his London collaborator. By February 1796 he was probably glad to stop. Exhausting though his CRT experience had been, it had proved 'very gainful', at least according to Hannah More. Besides, he had plenty of other printing work on hand, including a children's novel, *Easter Holidays*, the first of several books he came to publish for Althea Fanshawe, another moralising writer. Later in 1796 he was displaying and selling fine prints in a commercial arrangement with Ackermann or some other art house in London. Perhaps Hazard did after all exhibit business acumen.

Gye, Meyler and others, 1792-1795

In the early 1790s William Gye removed from outlying Westgate Buildings to the Marketplace, a better site for his stationery and printing shop and conveniently near the Guildhall with which he often had dealings. An overseer of the Abbey parish poor, he continued to interest himself in social issues and good causes, which in turn had business advantages. He printed the Bath freemen's legal case against Corporation in 1792 [title-page below, Fig.49], and from 1793 championed the interests of the new working men's benefit clubs by representing their members at the Quarter Sessions and revising and printing their rules – some copies apparently printed on satin. Seizing another opportunity, in early 1794 he opened a 'militia office', insuring subscribers against having to serve in the county militia. But what raised Gye's profile still higher that year was his issue of specially minted trade tokens with ha'penny and penny values. If the ostensible purpose here was to ease the chronic shortage of coin, it was a publicity coup as well. Not only did the circulating tokens signal his public spiritedness, but the penny token – bearing a charitable image and the legend 'Remember the Debtors in Ilchester Gaol' – advertised the cause always dearest to his heart.

SUBSTANCE

OF A

BILL in CHANCERY,

FILED AGAINST THE

Corporation of BATH,

BY THE

Committee of Freemen,

WITH THE

Anfwer of the Corporation.

GYE, PRINTER.

Fig.49

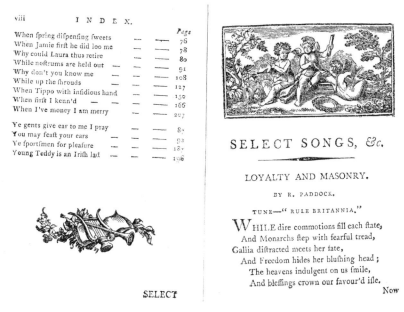

SELECT

SELECT SONGS, &c.

LOYALTY AND MASONRY.

BY R. PADDOCK.

TUNE—"RULE BRITANNIA."

WHILE dire commotions fill each state,
And Monarchs step with fearful tread,
Gallia distracted meets her fate,
And Freedom hides her blushing head;
The heavens indulgent on us smile,
And blessings crown our favour'd isle.
Now

Fig.50

William Meyler meanwhile remained preoccupied with the *Bath Herald*, which Paddock still printed from Green Street along with such occasional items as the song collection *The Apollo* – to whose 1794 edition Paddock made his own loyal, masonic contribution [Fig.50 above reduced]. In summer 1795 all this changed. Paddock gave up printing at Bath for an innkeeper's life at Taunton, to be replaced in Green Street by George Robbins with whom he had some (family?) connection. Robbins rather surprisingly equipped himself with the presses and type once belonging to J.Johnson, printer of the defunct *Bath Register*, rather than take over Paddock's, which went to auction later in the year. And while this was going on, Meyler sprang a surprise of his own. In June 1795 he bought out the other *Herald* shareholders to become the journal's sole proprietor, and, no longer having Paddock to print it, proceeded to set up a new press under his own control, in Kingston Buildings close to his Orange Grove bookshop. Was George Steart, Cruttwell's former apprentice, involved? Since leaving Cruttwell's Steart had worked as a self-employed printer and stationer in Beaufort Square, but Meyler was certainly using him that July to collect outstanding *Herald* debts. Steart himself also toyed with etching. His impression of coffee-house connoisseurs [detail below, Fig.51] comes from Edward Harington's curious effusion, *A Schizzo on the Genius of Man*, printed by Cruttwell in 1793.

Fig.51

Cruttwell in the 1790s

Of all Cruttwell's output the *Bath Chronicle* was perhaps the least financially profitable. Notifying his readers in December 1791 that the Bath newspapers would cost 4d. in future because of stamp duty, he explained that the country press had resisted passing on the 1789 increase for over two years, but the burden had become too great. What with tax, the penny commission allowed to agents, the cost of paper, and the losses on wasted stamped sheets, he had been running at a deficit – on top of which he was owed several hundred pounds by distant customers, some as far away as Ireland. Even nearer subscribers could be dilatory, as we know from Stephen Gay's plea for payment in 1791. Best known of all the travelling newsmen, Gay rode the area south of Bath in all weathers for nearly thirty years, carrying both the *Chronicle* and *Journal* as well as handbills, chapbooks, patent medicines, and at the New Year a specially printed address begging customers for a shilling tip.

In July 1797, with the country at war, an even harsher increase in stamp duty pushed newspaper prices up by 50%, to 6d. a copy. Meyler at the *Bath Herald* reacted stoically – the government needed the revenue – but Cruttwell was outraged, especially since the tax on advertisements had shot up too and would fall hardest on his most regular advertisers – auctioneers, booksellers and dealers in patent medicines. Newspaper circulations, he warned, were bound to suffer. Demand was not as inelastic as the government claimed. This was a tax on the freedom of the press. Yet all three Bath newspapers, *Chronicle*, *Journal* and *Herald*, survived.

Nor did the production of books ease off. Cruttwell printed 116 known books and pamphlets (of 24 pages and more) in the eight years 1791-1798. His total output was no doubt higher, but this suggests the scale. In terms of subject matter, 36% could be broadly classed as Religion, 15% Poetry and Fiction, 14% Current Affairs and Social Issues, 9% Medicine and Science, 8% History and Travel, with the remainder in various categories from Classics to Guidebooks. Many of these works were published in alliance with London bookseller/printers whose names appear on the title-pages, the contractual terms varying in each case from simple distribution agreements to actual printing commissions. Examples (with the bookseller's name added to each) included:

> Benjamin Hobhouse, *A Treatise on Heresy...* (1792) – Cadell
> Marcus Aurelius, *The Meditations...*, trans. Richard Graves (1792) – Robinson
> *A Liberal Version of the Psalms...*, trans. by W.R.Wake (1793) – Robinson/Dilly
> Daniel Neal, *The History of the Puritans...*, new ed. in 5 vols (1793) – Dilly/Johnson
> F.T.Travell, *The Duties of the Poor* (1793) – Rivington
> John Ewart, *Two Cases of... Cancer of the Mamma...* (1794) – Dilly
> Ann Wingrove, *Letters, Moral and Entertaining* (1795) – Wallis
> Robert Lovell and Robert Southey, *Poems* (1795) – Dilly
> H.Goudemetz, *Historical Epochs of the French Revolution* (1796) – Dilly
> William Wainhouse, *Poetical Essays (Latin and English)* (1796) – Dilly
> Benjamin Constant, *Observations on... the.... Government of France* (1797) – Robinson John
> John Billingsley, *General View of the Agriculture of Somerset*, rev. ed. (1797) – Dilly
> Charlotte Sanders, *The Little Family... for... young persons*, 2 vols (1797) – Dilly
> N.Brook, *Observations on the Manners... of Italy* (1798) - Cadell & Davies
> William Sole, *Menthae Britannicae... all the British Mints* (1798) – White

These presented different levels of publishing risk. Wake's edition of the *Psalms*, Wingrove's *Letters*, and Wainhouse's *Poetical Essays* were all backed by subscription lists. The volumes by the *émigré* Goudemetz (translated by Francis Randolph, a fashionable preacher at Bath) and by Billingsley (which had already proved itself in a London-printed edition) were both underwritten by their authors, but could in any case be expected to sell well. On the other hand, a 139-page collection of verse by two dreamy young Bristolians - Lovell and Southey's *Poems* [Fig.52 opposite] – was much more of a speculation even if Cruttwell was aware that the future Lake poet Southey had lived as a child at Bath. Charlotte Sanders's 2-volume *The Little Family* was probably a safer bet from Cruttwell's and Dilly's point of view because the market for children's literature was expanding all the time.

In addition to books distributed primarily through London, Cruttwell printed many items for local consumption. Some of these were undertaken at the request of institutions. On behalf of the Bath & West of England Agricultural Society he produced further volumes in the series of *Letters and Papers*, and in 1796 printed Anthony Fothergill's prize *Essay on the Abuse of Spirituous Liquors* for the Society to circulate to its members. He likewise printed for the Bath General Hospital and the Bath Casualty Hospital, taking over responsibility for the latter's annual report from Hooper & Keene. Thanks to his personal Anglican affiliations and the repute of the Bishop Wilson *Bible*, Cruttwell was also the first choice of many local churchmen with sermons, occasional verse, and other material for publication – a mixed category that took in doctrinal controversy, campaigning addresses in support of a new church in Walcot, an episcopal charge to the clergy of Durham, a psalter, a sentimental poem, or an amusing skit on the Greek motto recently fixed to the front of the Pump Room. Profits from this latter item – *Warm Water*, by the curate of St Michael's, W.R.Wake – went to the Puerperal Charity at Bath. It was not uncommon for other good causes to benefit in the same way from local publishing – the hospitals and infirmary, the Sunday schools, and the gaoled debtors. The Pauper Charity received the profits from one especially striking instance of vanity publishing in the service of philanthropy – the four successive volumes compiled by Sir John and Lady Anna Miller, and printed by Cruttwell, under the title under *Poetical Amusements at a Villa near Bath* (1775-81) – see earlier [page 41].

[54]

Fierce as their torrents, wily as the snake
That sharps his venom'd tooth in every brake,
Aloft the dreadful tomahawk they rear;
Patient of hunger, and of pain,
Close in their haunts the chiefs remain,
And lift in secret stand the deadly spear.
Yet, should the unarm'd traveller draw near,
And proffering forth the friendly hand,
Claim their protection from the warrior band;
The savage Indians bid their anger cease,
Lay down the ponderous spear, and give the pipe of
  peace.

Such virtue Nature gives: when man withdraws
To fashion's circle, far from nature's laws,
  How chang'd, how fall'n the human breast!
Cold Prudence comes, relentless foe!
Forbids the pitying tear to flow,
  And steels the soul of apathy to rest;
Mounts in relentless state her stubborn throne,
And deems of other bosoms by her own.

BION.

Fig.52

Publishing the antiquities

In September 1790, reporting the spectacular Roman stone carvings found during excavations for the new Pump Room, Cruttwell's *Bath Chronicle* noted that the city architect Thomas Baldwin was having them accurately drawn – with a view to publication. Thomas Pownall too was making drawings, and a few months later sent a description and drawing to the Society of Antiquaries with a warning not to publish details because of Baldwin's prior claim. Baldwin, however, produced nothing. Compromised financially, he eventually lost his official positions and was in 1794 declared bankrupt. Having 'withheld', as he put it, for four years Pownall decided to go ahead with his own plans.

Pownall, a former governor of Massachusetts and ex-M.P. for Minehead, had once written a treatise on the study of antiquities as well as descriptions of the antiquities of southern France. Against the general view that the excavated Bath stonework came from a temple of Minerva, he advanced a different opinion, that it belonged instead to a Sun temple. His slim quarto arguing the case, *Descriptions and Explanations of some Roman Antiquities dug up at Bath*, came out in 1795, printed and published by Cruttwell but with London booksellers also involved. It contained one fold-out plate [detail below, Fig.53] engraved by John Hibbert junior (son perhaps of the long-established Bath engraver William Hibbert) who had just returned from a three-year study tour to Italy. The same year Pownall got Cruttwell to print for him a more substantial book, *Intellectual Physics*, a grand cosmological disquisition that in due course required a second edition – unlike the *Antiquities* whose thesis Richard Warner had meanwhile demolished.

His position as curate of St James's church still left Warner ample time to indulge his passion for local history. Critical of Pownall's conjectures and even more dismayed by the physical neglect of the Roman fragments since their discovery, he conceived the idea, as he recalled later, 'not only of attempting their rescue... but of exalting them, through the medium of the press, into public notice'. This was the first step towards creating a public museum, near the Cross Bath, to house the city-owned antiquities, with an official catalogue, written by Warner himself, and sanctioned, published and paid for by the Corporation. In normal circumstances Cruttwell would surely have been asked to print this, but Cruttwell was the esteemed Governor Pownall's printer, so perhaps out of delicacy the Corporation turned to William Meyler instead. This decision was to cause Warner endless trouble.

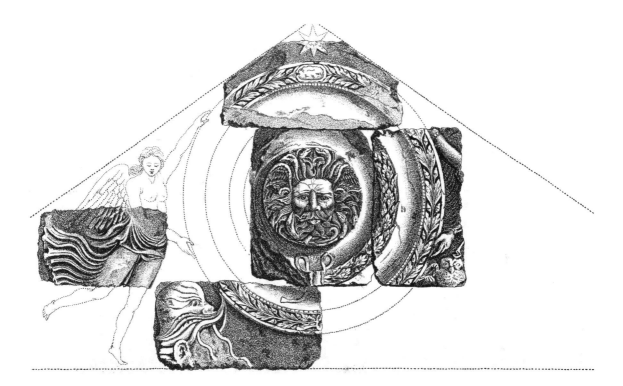

Fig.53

Fig.54

Many years later Warner described the scenario. Although Meyler may have employed a separate compositor on the *Bath Herald*, he had only 'one compositor for general business'- a pallid, gin-drinking, ill-educated man with a hand tremor that made him clumsy at setting type. In vain did Warner correct each proof and revise – 'the correction of one mistake invariably produced the appearance of two' – until in the end he gave up, 'leaving it to chance and the compositor'. When *An Illustration of the Roman Antiquities discovered at Bath* appeared at last in 1797, Warner estimated it contained some 150 errata. More striking were its illustrations [Fig.54 above]. Rather than commission the usual copperplates, Warner preferred the increasingly fashionable medium of white-line wood engraving, which had the advantage that the blocks could be printed simultaneously with the type and hence did not require a rolling press. A title-page vignette, signed 'Whitley – Bath', revealed the identity of the otherwise obscure engraver [see page 113].

Warner's actual text ranged more widely than Pownall's and of course he insisted, against Pownall, that the temple was dedicated to Minerva, represented by a Medusa head, and not to Sol. In Warner's words it was a matter of judgment. 'We fought the battle fairly before the public; left them to decide...'. His own book, though, won general approval, and led directly to his next, more ambitious work, *The History of Bath*. Cruttwell was this time fully involved, shouldering indeed the entire project, doing the printing, paying for the engravings, subsidising Warner's research and offering him royalties on top. First announced in May 1797, the *History* came out in January 1801, seen through the press by R.S.Cruttwell after his father's death, and with a flattering dedication to the Prince of Wales.

Decorations

Unlike illustrations, which the author furnished, commissioned, or at least approved, decorations belonged to the page lay-out and thus appeared largely at the whim of the printer. This selection suggests how Bath's Georgian printers used their opportunity.

Fig.55.*Clockwise from top left*
Factotum (woodblock initial with inserted type character), B.Lyons, 1730 --- Tailpiece, Thomas Boddely, 1746 --- Tailpiece, Stephen Martin, 1762 --- Tailpiece, Samuel Hazard, 1772 --- Tailpiece, Richard Cruttwell, 1785 --- Headpiece, Richard Cruttwell.

Fig.56. *Clockwise from top left*
Headpiece and tailpiece from same opening, Samuel Hazard, 1790 --- Tailpiece, Samuel Hazard, 1793 ---
Tailpiece, William Meyler, 1797 --- Headpiece from a *Koran*, Samuel Hazard, 1795 --- Headpiece and tailpiece
from same opening, William Meyler, 1799 --- Tailpiece, R.S.Cruttwell, 1801 --- Tailpiece, John Browne, 1815
--- Tailpiece from a poem *The Flagellator*, Benjamin Higman, 1815.

Natural history

Hazard and Cruttwell were both associated with botanical works of some note in the 1790s. It was not Hazard's first foray into this area. In 1778 he had printed the 168 engraved octavo plates and descriptions of John Walcott's *Flora Britannica Indigena*, originally issued in parts and then bound up with a frontispiece that included a vignette of the great Swedish taxonomist Linnaeus [Fig.57 below]. This was a derivative work compared with Walcott's other book on local fossils [see Fig.36] and certainly when set against the two slim folios on seaweeds that Hazard undertook in 1795 – the first monographs ever published on British algae.

Thomas Velley's *Coloured Figures of Marine Plants* distilled his spare-time research on seaweeds when stationed as a militia officer on wartime duty on the south coast. Besides the five hand-coloured printed plates, the text included an essay on the propagation of seaweeds. This particularly interested the second author, John Stackhouse, who had himself experimented with propagation in tanks of sea water at his house in Cornwall. Only the first part of his own monograph, *Nereis Britannica*, appeared in 1795 followed by two further parts, again printed by Hazard, in 1797 and 1801 for the London publisher, J.White. All contained etched plates after Stackhouse's watercolour drawings and subsequently hand-coloured by an unnamed female artist. To judge from the rare surviving copies the full complement seems to have been 24 plates [Fig.58 opposite]. What was more important about the publication was Stackhouse's creation of many new genera of seaweeds in a bold break with the hitherto accepted Linnaean classification, even though wider acceptance of his proposals must have been hampered by poor sales of parts 2-3. Not until 1816 did he issue a revised version, and this – like his other later works – was printed in Oxford despite his retirement to Bath in 1806. The one exception was a 32-page illustrated pamphlet that Hazard's successor, John Binns, printed for him in 1815, *Extracts from Bruce's Travels in Abyssinia... respecting the Balsam and Myrrh Trees*, an offshoot from his study of Ancient Greek botany.

In 1799 Hazard completed another botanical work, *The British Garden: a Descriptive Catalogue of Hardy Plants*, published anonymously but in fact compiled by a Bath resident, Lady Charlotte Murray. It ran to over 800 octavo pages in two volumes and lacked illustrations, yet rapid initial sales encouraged a second edition the same year. This must have fared less well since the unsold copies appear to have been recycled nine years later in a third edition from a different London publisher.

Two other significant botanical works of 1799, both by a well-known Bath apothecary, William Sole, were printed by Cruttwell. One, an illustrated account of British grasses, came out in the ninth volume of *Letters and Papers*, the journal Cruttwell had long published on behalf of the Bath & West Agricultural

Fig.57

Society. The other was an independent monograph on the mints, *Menthae Britannicae*, based on Sole's systematic investigations of this plant family in his own botanic garden rather than relying on Linnaeus, an approach that soon put him at odds with Sir J.E.Smith, president of the Linnean Society. It was a striking publication all the same, a Super Royal quarto on Whatman wove paper offering 24 full-plate etchings, all executed by William Hibbert from drawings by half-a-dozen different artists. One copy now at Kew was apparently printed in green with extra hand-colouring, despite the evidence that Sole thought colour only spoiled black-and-white illustrations.

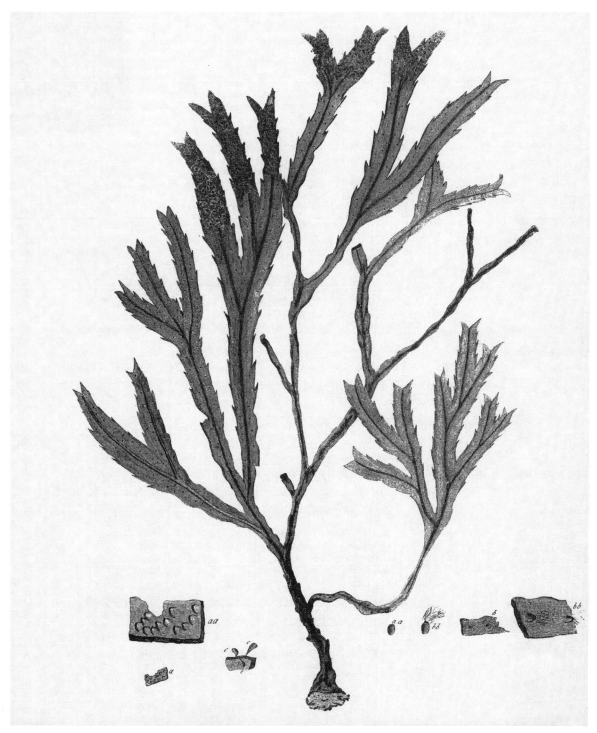

Fig.58

The old guard passes

Death claimed several of the city's leading printers around 1800. The firm of Hooper & Keene (latterly Hooper & Keenes) suffered most with the loss of Thomas Keene, John Keene and John Hooper, all within fourteen months, 1798-9. Ann Keene, Thomas's widow, considered herself heir to the business and declared at once that she would continue to publish the *Bath Journal* – from 7 Kingsmead Street as usual – with her elder son's assistance. Her precise legal claim was unclear all the same, and after years of family dispute – during which time the *Journal* was conducted by a business partner, Thomas Wood – the case went to the Court of Chancery for a decision.

John Hooper's death had been shortly preceded by that of his old *Bath Chronicle* rival Richard Cruttwell, who died at Cheltenham after a long illness in June 1799, aged only 52. Obituary notices dwelt on Cruttwell's thirty-year career, his high ranking among provincial printers, and the lasting fame of his Wilson *Bible*. Financially too he had done well. Besides the spacious St James's Street house and printing office (which he had had extended), he held property in Stall Street and elsewhere. He had estimated only in 1797 that the *Bath Chronicle* was worth £4000 and that his estate could afford to pay out £1200 in annuities. Nor was the inheritance or succession in doubt. Cruttwell's eldest son, 24-year-old Richard Shuttleworth Cruttwell, was the natural choice, and indeed he must have increasingly taken charge during his father's fatal illness. Throughout this seamless transition the production line never faltered. At least fifteen books rolled off the Cruttwell presses in 1799 and again in 1800, and the *Chronicle* came out in its normal fashion.

Over at William Gye's printing office in the Marketplace output was generally confined to jobbing work, broken only by the occasional pamphlet or full-scale book. Among these was a notable publication of 1800, *The Trial of Mrs.Jane Leigh Perrot... at Somerset Assizes... on a Charge of Stealing Lace*, i.e. the notorious case of Jane Austen's aunt in which Gye was personally embroiled as a potential witness for the prosecution. The premature death of his eldest son, William England Gye, in 1797 may have delayed any further expansion, but another son, Frederick Gye, was sufficiently practised in the trade by 1802 when William Gye died suddenly of apoplexy. A huge congregation attended the funeral, a testament to his philanthropic reputation. His widow Mary assumed responsibility for the business along with Frederick. This arrangement lasted until about 1806 when Frederick quitted Bath to found the printing firm of Gye & Balne in London. By then a further son, Henry Gye, had reached the age of twenty and was fully trained in printing. Under Mary Guy's proprietorship the presses had become busier, with half-a-dozen or more titles just from 1805.

William Gye had been unusually prominent in public affairs, but other printers also played their part. By 1800 R.S.Cruttwell had become a Bath Commissioner, Samuel Hazard was treasurer to the charitable Strangers' Friend Society, and in 1801 William Meyler won election to the City Council and later served as Constable and Sheriff. Meyler still produced Bath's third newspaper, the *Herald*, but restrained his book output to three or so titles a year – probably composed and printed in the gaps of the regular cycle of newspaper production, and all in tandem with his Orange Grove bookshop, library and lottery office. Although Hazard similarly had a bookshop and library to run, he contrived to print more, averaging at least ten publications annually in the seven years 1797-1803. One unexpected example, the 360-page story *Leonard & Gertrude* by the Swiss educationist J.H.Pestalozzi (1800) is illustrated opposite [Fig.59]. And in a similar vein came a series of short cautionary tales for young people by Althea Fanshawe, whose successful novel *Easter Holidays* he had first printed in 1797. Pious homilies and devotional works remained the overwhelming staple of the Hazard press – from the sermons of William Jay, the charismatic preacher at Argyle Chapel, to repeated editions of Henry Venn's *The Complete Duty of Man*. Yet Hazard printed much else – the verse of his old favourite Christopher Anstey still, *A View of Dublin* (c.1799), *A Candid Inquiry into the Education... of a Surgeon-Apothecary* (1800), and the botanical works described above – to go no further.

Besides the well-entrenched quintet of Keene, Cruttwell, Gye, Meyler and Hazard, two relative newcomers also competed for attention – John Browne and George Robbins. A self-proclaimed printer and bookseller, Browne had purchased a going bookshop concern in George Street in 1797, but concentrated at first on the retail trade and circulating library, indeed becoming prominent enough in these fields to be chosen librarian of a learnèd Bath subscription library set up in 1801. The same year his printing ambitions became clearer. No longer content with a solely jobbing role, he printed Richard Graves's *Senilities* for two London booksellers and, rather more significantly, launched the first of a new guidebook series, *The Historic and Local New Bath Guide*, issued in printed blue covers and with a smart engraved frontispiece [Fig.60 overleaf]. Though it contained more information than the long-existing *New Bath Guide*, printed by Cruttwell for the bookseller William Taylor, it was at 2s.6d. decidedly more expensive than Taylor's guide which sold for a shilling.

Nevertheless it was a sure way of attracting notice, as George Robbins had just demonstrated with his directory. Successor to Paddock, Robbins had spent over four years in Green Street (first at no.15 then at 20) before moving shop in early 1800 to 9 Bridge Street, next door to the engraver William Hibbert. Here he added art materials and prints – items sold by the previous occupant – to his usual stock of almanacs, prayer books, dictionaries, schoolbooks, and everyday stationery. He welcomed any sort of printing work 'particularly Books and Pamphlets, Catalogues, Posting-Bills, Hand-Bills, Cards with elegant and fashionable Borders, &c. &c.'. But in practice he seems to have undertaken nothing more substantial than the odd pamphlet – until 1800, that is, when he underlined his move to Bridge Street by bringing out *Robbins' Bath Directory*, a serious piece of research on his part and the fullest list of local residents yet published, though of course omitting the poor.

In printing his directory Robbins still employed the 'long s' – just as Hazard did in the example below. After 1800, however, one by one the Bath printers gradually abandoned the 'long s' as old-fashioned. Like the marked reduction in the use of uppercase initials and less idiosyncratic punctuation, this was another sign of the typographical innovation also evident in the growing popularity of 'modern' faces, fancy display type, and experimental lay-out. Fig.61 overleaf, Hazard's title-page design for Edward Sheppard's obituary verses exhibits a self-conscious austerity in keeping with the book's contents only marred by the slightly misaligned 'BATH' wood block.

286

So saying, he slipped out of the room and disappeared.

Chapter the Seventy-third.

The Landmark.

COLLINS remained for a time speechless : his eyes rolled in his head ; he foamed at the mouth ; he trembled ; he stamped about : and at last called to his wife : " Bring me the brandy-bottle : it is resolved ; I'll go this instant."
Wife. Where then ? where do you mean to go in this dark night ?
Steward. I will go : I am resolved nothing shall stop me. I'll remove the stone. Give me the brandy.
Wife. For Heaven's sake, think what you are about !
Steward. No matter ; go I will, that's flat.
Wife. It is so dark, you cannot see your hand before you ! It's almost midnight ; and besides it's Holy Week, when the devil is more mischievous than common.
Steward. In for a penny, in for a

287

pound : give me my bottle, and I'll be off.
So saying, he took a pickaxe, a spade, and a gavlock upon his shoulder ; and notwithstanding the darkness, he hurried away towards the mountain, in order to remove the stone that marked the boundaries of the lordship. He was already heated with liquor, and inflamed with rage, which made him valiant. Still at the motion of every leaf, and at every sound, he shuddered : but pressing forward, he reached the boundary, and began immediately to hack, and dig round it to get it loose.

Chapter the Seventy-fourth.

Darkness, and the night, ill suit an evil Conscience.

WHILE he was thus occupied, he heard a noise that alarmed him ; and all of a sudden a black man appeared behind him amongst the bushes. His figure shone amidst the darkness of the night, and a flame proceeded from his head. It immediately occurred to the steward, that it must

Fig.59

VIEW of the PUMP-ROOM, BATH.

Publish'd Nov.ʳ 5. 1802

THE
HISTORIC & LOCAL

NEW BATH GUIDE:

Informing and useful to *Travellers*, and those who visit or reside
in this ancient City.

CONTAINING

An Account of the FIRST DISCOVERY of the MEDICINAL
VIRTUES of its *WATERS*, by King BLADUD;

The Origin of BATH, and of Historic Facts from the Year of our Lord 44:

Roman and Saxon Antiquities.

A DESCRIPTION OF THE

Churches, Chapels, & other Buildings for public Worship :
HOSPITALS, and other CHARITABLE INSTITUTIONS :

Also of the Squares, Circus, Crescents, Parades, principal Streets,
and Public Edifices.

The BATH WATERS, Cause of their Heat, Virtues, &c.

AN ACCOUNT OF THE

Corporation,	Libraries,	Baths,
Courts of Judicature,	Newspapers,	Bridges,
Representation,	Arms,	River,
Number of Houses	Markets,	Quay,
and Inhabitants,	Fairs,	Coals, &c. &c.

A Description of the Pump-Room, Assembly-Rooms,
Theatre, Sydney-Gardens, *& other Places of Amusement.*

Biographical Sketch of Rich. Nash, Esq.

Who presided over the Amusements in this City upwards of 50 Years.

ALSO LISTS OF THE

Body Corporate,	Bankers,	Lodging-houses,	Coaches,
Medical Faculty,	Artists,	Chairmens'Fares	Waggons,
Attornies,	Inns & Taverns	Post & Carriers,	Barges, &c.

LIKEWISE,

An Account of the City of Bristol, the Hotwells, & Clifton,
AND A CONCISE HISTORY OF CHELTENHAM;

Gentlemen's Seats, &c. in the Vicinity of BATH,

The principal Roads to different Parts of the Kingdom, with the
Distances,

And a Variety of other Particulars worthy Observation.

[Adorned with PLATES and CUTS.]

BATH : Published and Sold by J. BROWNE, *George-Street.*
Sold also by other Booksellers in Bath ; T. Hurst, London ; and by
R. Edwards, Printer, *Broad-Street,* Bristol.

Fig.60

L I N E S

ON THE

𝕯eath of a much-loved 𝕾ister.

OCTOBER, 1795.

⊛ B A T H ⊛

Printed by S. HAZARD, 1797.

Fig.61

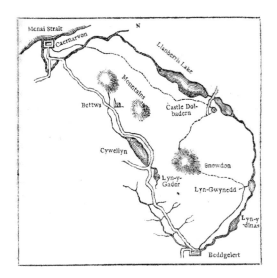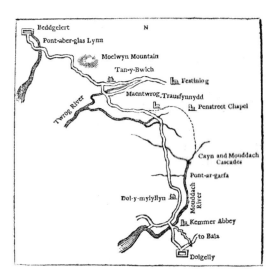

Fig.62

The Cruttwells and Rev. Richard Warner

When Warner became curate of St James's church in 1794, he quickly struck up a close friendship with Richard Cruttwell senior, one of his churchwardens and from 1796 his regular printer. Apart from all else they shared political views. Cruttwell – unlike his Tory brother William Cruttwell at the *Sherborne Journal* - was a Whig, though never flaunting the fact in the *Bath Chronicle*. The *Chronicle* office, a few steps from St James's church, was nevertheless rumoured to be a meeting-place for political sympathisers, Warner among them.

The friendship was further cemented in 1797 when Cruttwell agreed to finance Warner's research for *The History of Bath*, and also saw his 22-year-old son, R.S.Cruttwell, set out with Warner on an 18-day, 462-mile tour of Wales, which provided the material for *A Walk through Wales* published in 1798. Inspired by the well-known 'picturesque' tours of William Gilpin and adorned with a romantic aquatint of Tintern Abbey, Warner's volume was a pleasantly anecdotal guide that offered readers a useful engraved sketch of each day's ramble [examples above, Fig.62]. The Tintern aquatint was executed in London by Samuel Alken, but Cruttwell may well have entrusted the small maps to the Bath engraver William Gingell, who certainly produced the map of the Holy Land for Warner's life of Christ, *The English Diatessaron*, a few years later. The book of the Welsh tour, running into four editions by 1800, meanwhile brought Warner some fame and soon led to sequels, beginning with *A Second Walk through Wales* issued in 1799. This time his companions were another of Cruttwell's sons, the 18-year-old Clement, and an ex-officer of the French revolutionary army who on one occasion on the tour sang the 'Marseillaise' to joint approval, an almost treasonable act in the 1790s. As to the book, the winning formula of diary-like text, small engraved maps, and the odd Alken aquatint, was retained in this and subsequent volumes – *A Walk through... the Western Counties* (1800), *Excursions from Bath* (1801), and *A Tour through the Northern Counties... and the Borders of Scotland* (2 vols, 1802) [aquatint opposite, Fig.63] – all printed by the Cruttwells *père et fils* in a deliberately uniform style. Only the London publishing house changed, switching from Dilly to G. & J.Robinson.

Warner's prolific output fell into three main groups – the travel books (with a Cornish tour added in 1809), the sermons and religious works, and various items of mainly Bath interest. The sermons included three collected editions – *Practical Discourses* (2 vols, 1803-4), *Scripture Characters* (2 vols, 1810-11), and *Sermons, Tracts and Notes...* (3 vols, 1813), but the individually published sermons and addresses (often published to benefit good causes) were equally important and sometimes hard-hitting. Several of his St James's congregation walked out during a sermon on frivolous life-styles (printed in 1806 as *The Overflowings of Ungodliness*), and his provocative fast-day sermon in May 1804, *War Inconsistent with Christianity*, became notorious. Preached to an audience that included a contingent of local militia and later dedicated to Charles James Fox, the Whig leader, it was written with publication in mind, the text being handed over to R.S.Cruttwell in the vestry immediately after delivery. It went through six editions, stirred up what Warner called a 'paper war', and maybe profited Cruttwell more than Warner's earnest life of Christ (1803), or prayer book (1806).

Whether Cruttwell recouped all his considerable costs in funding Warner's *A History of Bath* (1801) is an open question, given the research involved and the generous production – over 500 pages in Royal quarto format, printed with new type on hot-pressed vellum wove, and very decently illustrated. The venture was at least buttressed by advance subscription, so that sales were unaffected by a hostile notice of the work in the *Critical Review* that Warner claimed was politically motivated. Although there would be no second edition of the *History*, Warner's main London bookseller G.& J.Robinson (later Wilkie & Robinson) did publish two spin-offs, *An Historical and Descriptive Account of Bath* (1802) and *A New Guide through Bath* (1811), both printed as usual by Cruttwell. The 1811 work reproduced, without acknowledgment, William Smith's 'fossilogical map' revealing the geology five miles around Bath, and Warner has been labelled a plagiarist for doing so. But since Warner knew Smith well, dedicated the book to the Mayor and Corporation, and openly made the map a selling point in press advertisements, it seems unlikely he never obtained Smith's permission.

Fig.63

Alongside the antiquary, the Bible scholar, the preacher, the traveller, there existed a more satirical Warner who hid behind pseudonyms – Peter Paul Pallet, Timothy Goosequill, and Gabriel Sticking-Plaister – or else, in the case of the newsmens' addresses done for the *Bath Chronicle*, remained anonymous. His *Rebellion in Bath, or The Battle of the Upper* [Assembly] *Rooms* appeared in two 'heroico-odico-tragico-comico' cantos in 1808-9. The public guessed in vain at the author of this and its predecessor, *Bath Characters, or Sketches from Life*, a series of dialogues featuring transparently disguised notabilities. Wisely their printer went unnamed as well. It was probably not Cruttwell – who was, however, concerned in one of Warner's subsequent light-hearted forays, *Omnium-Gatherum*, still to be discussed [see page 85].

Fig.64

29

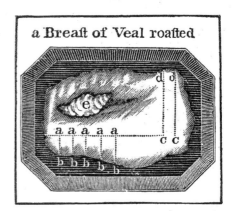

a Breaſt of Veal roaſted

carved, should be first cut down quite through, in the first line on the left, *d, c;* it should next be cut, across in the line, *a, c,* from *c,* to the last *a,* on the left, quite through dividing the gristle from the rib-bones; this done to those who like fat and gristle, the thick or gristly part should be cut into pieces, as wanted, in the lines *a, b.* When a breast of veal is cut into pieces and stewed, these gristles are very tender, and eatable. To such persons as prefer a bone, a rib should be cut or separated from the rest, in the line *d, c,* and with a part of the breast, a slice of the sweet-bread, *e,* cut across the middle.

Fig.65

THE

𝕭𝖆𝖙𝖍 𝕾𝖔𝖓𝖌𝖘𝖙𝖊𝖗,

BEING A COLLECTION OF

THE NEWEST SONGS,

LATELY SUNG AT

THE THEATRES, VAUXHALL,

HARMONIC SOCIETIES, &c. &c.

ALSO,

A Collection of Toasts and Sentiments.

BATH:
Printed and sold by M. Gye, Market-Place;

AND SOLD BY

The Booksellers of Bath and Bristol, and Messrs.
Champante and Whitrow, London.

Fig.66

Mary Gye, 1802-1809

The four illustrations here convey some idea of the work carried out by Frederick Gye (until c.1806) and then Henry Gye under the widowed Mary Gye's management. Fig.64 opposite, the woodcut frontispiece to *Narrative Sketches of the Conquest of Mysore* (4th ed., 1803) advertises a touring panorama painting, Robert Ker Porter's 'The Storming of Seringapatam'. Next to it [Fig.65] is a page printed in bold type from the 5th edition of John Trusler's *The Honours of the Table... with the Whole Art of Carving* (c.1807). Trusler, author of a bewildering variety of books (and himself a one-time London printer) probably brought the woodblocks from earlier editions with him when he retired to Bath. He employed the Gye press on several other publications at this period but turned to another printer, John Browne, for the first instalment of his *Memoirs* in 1806. The songbook on the left [Fig.66] dates from around 1805. Like the various other song- and hymn-books produced at Bath over the years, it contained no music. The fourth Gye example [Fig.67 below] illustrates the popular genre of trial literature – in this instance the topical case of James Taylor, tried at the Taunton Assizes in 1809 for a Bath murder. Not long before printing this Gye had acquired 'a peculiarly neat and genteel Assortment of TYPE, from the most distinguished Foundries' for bookwork, jobbing, and large, fancy display.

JAMES TAYLOR,

*Of the City of Bath, aged twenty-three years, was in-
dicted for the Wilful Murder of John Dyer, Coachman; to which he pleaded, " Not Guilty."*

*There were other indictments against him, to which he
also pleaded, " Not Guilty."*

COUNSEL FOR PROSECUTION.

Mr. MOORE, and Mr. LARPENT.

COUNSEL FOR PRISONER.

Mr. JEKYLL, Mr. BURROW, and Mr. EAST.

THE CASE being OPENED by Mr. MOORE

With a mere Narration of the Facts, the following Evidence was adduced in support of the Charge for the Wilful Murder of the aforesaid John Dyer.

William George Guion

DEPOSED that he was a Mail Coachman, and lived at Bath, that he knew the prisoner, and the deceased (Dyer) very well, that he (Guion) was rather deaf. The prisoner was no trade or profession, he lived with his mother Mrs. Roy, who keeps a public house called the Bell, in Stall Street, Bath; Robert Johnson a Mail Coachman, who drives the Bristol Mail into London, saw the prisoner on the twenty second of December last, at the Bell, (his mother's house) first saw him at 7 o'clock, or thereabouts. The witness and Johnson went into the house together, called for a pint of beer, about

A

Fig.67

Close of the Hazard era

Samuel Hazard, the city's longest-surviving individual printer, died in September 1806, having maintained his normal steady output of books and pamphlets to the end. Religious titles predominated as ever, exemplified by William Jay's 79-page missionary sermon below [Fig.68]. His largest printing commission from this period, however, may well have been Charles Mayo's *A Compendious View of Universal History... 1753 to... 1802* which ran to more than two thousand pages and came out in four volumes in 1804. Hazard had already taken his son-in-law and fellow-Moravian, John Binns, into partnership a year or two before his death, and from October 1806 Hazard's widow Ann continued the printing office, bookshop and circulating library for another three years as Hazard & Binns until the latter became sole proprietor. A handful of titles appeared under this joint imprint, including Mary Ward's *Original Poetry* in 1807, and the first part of Thomas Cogan's *An Ethical Treatise on the Passions* also printed in 1807 and completed in 1810 by Binns now on his own.

There were other comings and goings. George Robbins' toil over the *Bath Directory* (1800) won him few commissions – John Duncan's *Seasonable Hints* [top right reduced] a rare exception. In 1804

THE VALUE OF LIFE.

A

SERMON

delivered May 8th, 1803,

BEFORE

THE CORRESPONDENT BOARD IN LONDON

OF

THE SOCIETY IN SCOTLAND,

(INCORPORATED BY ROYAL CHARTER)

FOR THE PROPAGATION OF CHRISTIAN KNOWLEDGE

IN

THE HIGHLANDS AND ISLANDS.

By WILLIAM JAY.

Dum vivimus vivamus.

" Live while you live," the epicure would say,
" And seize the pleasures of the present day."
" Live while you live," the sacred preacher cries,
" And give to God each moment as it flies."
Lord, in my views let both united be ;
I live in *pleasure* when I live to *Thee.*

DODDRIDGE.

BATH:

PRINTED AND SOLD BY S.HAZARD,

IN CHEAP-STREET:

SOLD ALSO BY C.SMITH, BATH: T.WILLIAMS, STATIONERS COURT, LUDGATE-HILL; J. MATHEWS, STRAND; OGLE, GREAT TURNSTILE, HOLBORN; LONDON: OGLE AND AIKMAN, EDINBURGH: OGLE, GLASGOW: AND JAMES, BRISTOL.

1803.

Price 1s. 6d.

Fig.68

SEASONABLE HINTS,

TO THE

YOUNGER PART

OF

THE CLERGY,

OF THE

Church of England.

OCCASIONED. BY

THE RELATIVE INCREASE OF LIBERTINISM,

AND

THE ANTINOMIAN HERESY,

The Timely Clofe of the

WANSEY and BLAGDON CONTROVERSIES,

AND

THE REPORTED SUPPRESSION

OF

Methodift Conventicles, in the Diocefe of Salifbury.

Peace, Peace, for Shame, if not for Charity.
SHAKESPEARE.

The Profits of this Publication will be given to the Support of the decreafing
Fund of the School of Induftry, in the City of Bath.

By JOHN DUNCAN, D. D.

RECTOR OF SOUTH WARMBOROUGH, HANTS.

BATH:

PRINTED BY G. ROBBINS, BRIDGE-STREET,

FOR J. BARRATT, BOND-STREET;

And Sold by all the Bookfellers in Bath; Norton, and Browne, Briftol;
and Cadell and Davis, Strand, London.

1802.

Fig.69

he sold off his printing shop to John Savage, a book- and music-seller at 12 Argyle Street, who had acquired the publishing rights in Cruttwell's former *New Bath Guide*. The next three editions of the *Guide*, 1804-6, Savage printed himself, raising the price from a shilling to 1s.6d. to cover the extra duty on paper, and adding a couple more illustrations [e.g. the plate of Farleigh Hungerford castle, Fig.70]. He then disposed of Robbins' presses and stock of type to a jobbing printer, William Wimpey, and opened a circulating library instead, though continuing to publish the profitable *Guide*. Wimpey may have printed the 1807 and 1808 editions for him from the standing type, but from 1809 it turned into a joint publication with William Meyler. By then Wimpey had moved to Bathampton where his wife ran a girls' school. Despite his purchase of 'a vast quantity' of additional type, his jobbing business in Westgate Buildings had lasted for a mere fifteen months against the strong competition.

Fig.70

John Browne, *Le Papillon* and other magazines

Having launched the second Bath guidebook series in 1801, Browne kept it going with personally updated, new editions in 1805 and then 1809, by which time he had moved his bookshop and presses to Bridge Street – a good commercial location (like John Savage's bookshop and library in nearby Argyle Street) thanks to the recent expansion of Bathwick. Among the dozen or so titles attributable to him at this time (1801-9) was the curious *Life and Adventures of Bampfylde-Moore Carew* (1802), a racy account of the adoptive 'Gipsy King' whose frontispiece portrait appears below [Fig.71]. This seems to have been a joint publishing venture with the London booksellers Crosby & Letterman, who were also part of the consortium that commissioned Browne to print *Buonaparteana*, anecdotes of Napoleon's family, in 1804 – published on the heels of another Browne imprint concerning the invasion threatened by the resumption of the Napoleonic war. On his own initiative Browne also brought out a re-set, illustrated edition *of The New Bath Guide* – not an actual guide but Christopher Anstey's ever-popular doggerel satire – taking the view, no doubt, that Hazard's near monopoly on Anstey had expired with his death the year before. This came out in 1807 [Fig.72 below], with a reprint needed in 1809.

Fig.71

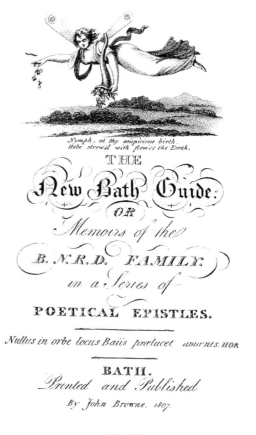

Fig.72

291

Monday, May the 8th, 1809.

A PEEP at the PUMP-ROOM:

(Continued from Page, 261.)

VISITOR.

What dashing Belle walks yonder, with that genteel young man in the blue great coat? I dont recollect
ever seeing her before.

INHABITANT.

Most probably not: she is like yourself, a stranger at
Bath; her name only appeared in the *last* Monday ar-
rivals. She will be better known ere she leaves it, I
make no doubt, and indeed a young woman of her
appearance is seldom *unnoticed* any where: Her name
is ROSALINDA LOVEKISS; she is from the Vicinity
of Bloomsbury-square, in London. This Lady is
the natural daughter of a Man of fashion, who dying
while she was only in her fifteenth year, left her in the
possession of a very large property, immediately at her
own disposal, with the sole restriction of not touching
the capital.

VISITOR.

Had she no guardians to direct or advise her in the
application of it?

P P

Fig.73

Early in 1809 Browne found himself a magazine printer. Sponsored by a 'Society of Literary Gentlemen', *Le Papillon, or The Fashionable Trifler and Bath Censor* started up on 23 January and ran for ten issues, sometimes fortnightly, sometimes weekly, until 8 May. Apart from some harsh words about the craven attitude of Bath's three newspapers, afraid to criticise anyone or anything for fear of giving offence, it was hardly the fierce censor it posed as. The excerpt from the final issue shown above [Fig.73] reveals the tone, steering well clear of the libellous comment that forced the speedy closure of a rival magazine, the *Ragnatello* (a spider's web to snare the butterfly, i.e. *le papillon*), whose printer and sponsors are unknown.

The history of magazine publishing at Bath was by no means illustrious. Cruttwell had been associated with several attempts in the 1770s – the two-page *Entertaining Miscellany* (1772-3, given away with the *Bath Chronicle*), the substantial *Monthly Miscellany* (1774-5, with London and Salisbury collaborators), the *Bath and Bristol Magazine* (1776, with Bristol collaborators), and the *Busy Body* (1778). These were all short-lived, as was *The Universal Museum*, 'a Magazine of Intelligence and Amusement', that Cruttwell briefly printed in 1791-2. Nor did later titles fare any better. *The Contemplator*, printed in 1812 by Meyler & Son for the Theatre Royal actor, William Abbott, seems to have foundered after one issue. *The West of England Magazine*, printed by Gye & Son for booksellers in Bath, Bristol and Taunton, presented itself as a serious miscellany covering economic, scientific and literary matters, but it too managed only six monthly numbers, January-June 1813. And similarly with Richard Warner's *Omnium-Gatherum*, which achieved just seven numbers in 1814-15. Only 150 copies sold of the 700 that Cruttwell hopefully printed of the first number and by the seventh and final number sales were down to 34.

Jobbing

The great standby of any general printer, jobbing was in a sense the creation of printed ephemera. Whereas books and most pamphlets, journals, and the like were meant to be kept, the typical product of jobbing was intended for some fairly immediate use and then to be discarded. Hence the word applied to utilitarian, small-scale, quickly executed work in a great range of formats from small tickets, visiting cards, and trade bills to folded leaflets, catalogues, and large wall posters. One important category comprised official forms of all sorts, administrative, legal and commercial – warrants, summonses, certificates, licences, contracts, insurance policies, shop bills, receipts, and many more. As a rule these would be part-printed or perhaps only headed, with space for completion in writing at the time of each transaction – as in the example below [Fig.74] showing Cruttwell's pre-printed bill for an advertisement in the *Bath Chronicle* made out to John Jefferys, the Town Clerk.

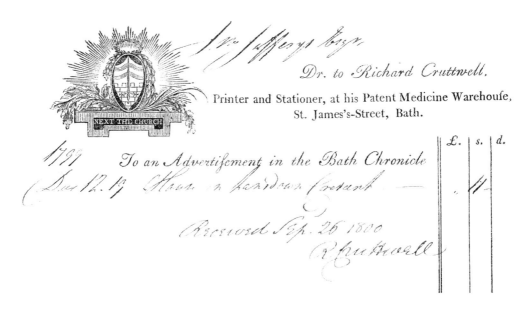

Fig.74

Even more miscellaneous was the whole class of hand-bills and public notices. One particularly good client was Bath's Theatre Royal, its frequent changes of programmes and casts creating a repeated demand for posters from those printers (Keene above all) able to do them at short notice – the poster illustrated opposite [Fig.75] certainly shows signs of hurried production. Handbills advertising balls, concerts, exhibitions, lectures, races, transport services, luxury goods, auction sales, charity events, and much else were pinned up in coffee houses and the Pump Room, fixed on buildings and (printed double-sided) on windows, and perhaps handed out on the streets. And clamouring for attention with all these were official notices and displays of rules and regulations – like Meyler's handsome broadsheet about prison donations partly illustrated overleaf [Fig.77]. Cruttwell, for instance, issued an account of the postal services on a large card, a 'Marketing Table for buying and selling' on a whole sheet or pasteboard, and 'Exhortations against Swearing, Drunkenness, and Sabbath-Breaking' on a half sheet. His report printed for the Batheaston Coal Company [detail overleaf, Fig.76, with William Smith's geological opinion] is representative, moreover, of the increasing amount of jobbing work carried out for companies, trusts, societies, charities, and other institutions. In this case the Cruttwells were personally concerned, both as shareholders in the coal company and because the printer's brother was its legal advisor. Annual reports often record payments to printers. One from the Bath Society of Guardians in 1795 thus specifies bills from Gye, Hooper & Keene, Cruttwell, and Paddock.

THEATRE-ROYAL, BATH.

The Last NIGHT of Mrs. SECOND's *ENGAGEMENT.*

This present TUESDAY, DECEMBER 6th, 1803,

Will be presented the COMIC OPERA of

THE DUENNA.

Don Jerome - - - - Mr. E D W I N.
Don Ferdinand - - - Mr. T A Y L O R.
Don Antonio - - - Mr. T E B A Y.
Don Carlos - - - - Mr. W E B B E R.
Father Paul - - - - Mr. B E N N E T T.
Father Augustine - - Mr. D O Y L E.
Isaac Mendoza - - - Mr. L O V E G R O V E.

The Duenna - - - Mrs. D I D I E R.
Donna Louisa - - Mrs. T A Y L O R.
Clara's Maid - - - Miss S U M M E R S.
Donna Clara (*with additional Songs*) Mrs. S E C O N D.

IN THE COURSE OF THE EVENING

(*By Particular Desire*)

Mrs. SECOND will Sing the Celebrated SONG of
CRAZY JANE, in Character.

To which will be added, the Favourite FARCE of The

DEAF LOVER.

Meadows - - - - - - Mr. ELLISTON.
Young Wrongward Mr. LANGDON. | Groom - - Mr. TEBAY.
Canteen - - Mr. CUNNINGHAM | William - - Mr. PARSONS.
Sternhold - - Mr. J. SMITH. | John - - - Mr. DOYLE.
Old Wrongward - - - - - Mr. EVANS.

Sophia - - Mrs. CUNNINGHAM. | Betsy Blossom - Mrs. TAYLOR.

On Thursday, PIZARRO; with BON TON.

On Saturday next the New Comedy of the MARRIAGE PROMISE, (which was received with the warmest
applause) will be repeated ; with the revived Musical Entertainment of The CAMP.

Doors to be opened at Quarter past Five o'Clock, and begin at a Quarter after Six.

Boxes, 4s.—Pit, 2s 6d.—First Gallery 1s. 6d.—Upper Gallery 1s.

Tickets and Places may be had of Mr. Bartley, at the Theatre, from Ten till Three.

Keenes, Printers, Kingsmead-Street.

Fig.75

Bath-Easton Coal Company.

THE Proprietors of this Concern having expended their original Subfcription, and being empowered by their Deed of Co-Partnerfhip to raife a further Sum of £5,000, by a Grant of 100 New Shares, at £50 each, (if fo much fhould be wanted;) and more than 50 of fuch new Shares having been engaged by the f...wing Subf...bers, the R... ...nder are n... offered to ...ou, and ... of ... S

Mr. SMITH's STATEMENT.

" The Strata already funk through for Coal at Bath-Eafton, and drawn in a Section, (fent herewith,) are undoubtedly the fame as thofe well known upon the Surface of many Hundred Acres of Land now working for Coal in the Counties of Glocefter and Somerfet.

" Thofe beneath the Bottom of the Pit already perforated by Boring to the Depth of 56 Feet, are alfo found in the fame regular Succeffion, as is well known in the Neighbourhood. By fuch Boring, alfo, the Strata now to be funk through are proved to be no harder than thofe ufually perforated for Coal. Thefe Borings have alfo further proved, that the Strata of Red Ground Mill-Stone, or Red Ground Stone, which at other Pits produces an immenfe Quantity of Water, does not here produce any. This very favourable Cir-cumftance, and the well-known Practicability of walling up all the prefent Water, are fingular Advantages. But independent of this Method of getting rid of the Water, the prefent very powerful Steam-Engine will enable the Sinkers to purfue their Work without Interruption, and very fhortly to exhibit ocular Proofs of the Strata which lead to Coal;* and which, I have no doubt, will moft fully juftify my former Expectations, and give the Proprietors the moft flattering Encouragement to purfue the Work."

The next General Meeting will be holden at the Gloucefter Inn, Bath, on Monday the 28th Inftant, at 11 o'Clock in the Forenoon.

P. S. The Sinking is now 28 Feet below the Source of the Water, which was in the Middle of the White Lias, a Circumftance *highly favourable.*

By Order of the Committee,

Thos. M. Cruttwell,
SOLICITOR.

Bath, March 7, 1808.

* The Strata funk through fince writing the above has completely verified this Affertion.

Richard Cruttwell, Printer, St. James's-Street, Bath.

Fig.76

MARCH 9th, 1808.

Guildhall, Bath.

𝔒𝔯𝔡𝔢𝔯𝔢𝔡—

THAT all Donations for the Prisoners confined in Bath Prison be from time to time, and without delay, reported to the Mayor and Sheriffs ; in order that, where the Case may require, Regulations may be ordained for the due Distribution thereof.

𝔒𝔯𝔡𝔢𝔯𝔢𝔡—

THAT in cases of Donations of Coals, per day (so long as any remain) be measured out and delivered for the use of the Common Room.

𝔒𝔯𝔡𝔢𝔯𝔢𝔡—

THAT such Coals be on no account made use of in any other Room or Rooms of, or belonging to, the said Prison, without a

Fig.77

אֵלַי קֹרֵא מִשֵּׂעִיר	To me one crieth out of Seir:
שֹׁמֵר מַה־מִלַּיְלָה	Watchman, what *report* of the night?
שֹׁמֵר מַה־מִלֵּיל :	Watchman, what of the night?
אָמַר שֹׁמֵר	12 The watchman saith,
אָתָא בֹקֶר וְגַם־לָיְלָה	Morning cometh; but still it is night.
אִם־תִּבְעָיוּן בְּעָיוּ שֻׁבוּ אֵתָיוּ :	If ye will enquire, enquire; return, come *to me.*
מַשָּׂא בַּעֲרָב	13 The oracle in the evening.
בַּיַּעַר בַּעֲרַב תָּלִינוּ	In the forest, at even, shall ye lodge,
אֹרְחוֹת דְּדָנִים :	O ye caravans of Dedan!
לִקְרַאת צָמֵא הֵתָיוּ מָיִם	14 To meet the thirsty, bring forth water,
יֹשְׁבֵי אֶרֶץ תֵּימָא	O inhabitants of the land of Tema!
בְּלַחְמוֹ קִדְּמוּ נֹדֵד :	With his *due of* bread prevent the fugitive.
כִּי־מִפְּנֵי חֲרָבוֹת נָדָדוּ	15 For from before the swords are they fled,
מִפְּנֵי חֶרֶב נְטוּשָׁה	From before the drawn sword,
וּמִפְּנֵי קֶשֶׁת דְּרוּכָה	And from before the bended bow,
וּמִפְּנֵי כֹּבֶד מִלְחָמָה :	And from before the pressure of war.
כִּי־כֹה אָמַר אֲדֹנָי אֵלָי	16 For thus hath the Lord said unto me:
בְּעוֹד שָׁנָה כִּשְׁנֵי שָׂכִיר	Within yet a year, as the years of an hireling,
וְכָלָה כָּל־כְּבוֹד קֵדָר :	Shall all the glory of Kedar end,
וּשְׁאָר מִסְפַּר־קֶשֶׁת גִּבּוֹרֵי	17 And the remnant of his numerous archery, the mighty men,
בְנֵי־קֵדָר יִמְעָטוּ	The sons of Kedar shall be diminished;
כִּי יְהוָה אֱלֹהֵי־יִשְׂרָאֵל דִּבֵּר :	For Jehovah, the God of Israel, hath said it.

R.S.Cruttwell and William Meyler, 1803-1809

The confident setting of Hebrew characters above comes from Cruttwell's *The Book of the Prophet Isaiah* in Joseph Stock's bilingual edition of 1803. Although several Bath printers had Greek founts, Cruttwell was probably the only one furnished with enough Hebrew type to carry out such a task – and likewise the important revision of *Robertson's Compendious Hebrew Dictionary*, announced in 1810 and finally achieved in 1814 under the close supervision of its editor, the Hebrew scholar Nahum Joseph. Occasional prestige imprints like these, a regular flow of other books and pamphlets, and the regular weekly manifestation of the *Bath Chronicle*, all assured Cruttwell of a comfortable lead over his competitors. He was virtually the house printer to certain authors (e.g. Richard Warner, the poet W.L.Bowles, the Bowdler family) and to various local institutions, and over the seven years 1803-9 he printed at least as many titles and new editions as all the other Bath printers put together. Some of these were of course relatively small beer – public addresses, sermons, annual reports, and the like – but others demanded far more effort in preparation, composition, presswork, binding up, and other operations. Elizabeth Hamilton's *Memoirs of the Life of Agrippina* (3 vols, 1804) ran to more than a thousand pages, and Thomas Percival's *Works, Literary, Moral and Medical* (new ed., 4 vols, 1807) to well over two thousand, to cite only two.

During this period William Meyler was printing no more than three or four books a year, yet in subject and style they covered quite as great a range as Cruttwell's. Three examples appear opposite. The statistical table [Fig.78] appeared in William Falconer's *A Practical Dissertation on the Medicinal Effects of Bath Water* (3rd ed., 1807), a title whose history went back to 1790 when Cruttwell printed the first edition on behalf of Meyler who had not yet established his press. Printed as well as published by Meyler this time, the enlarged third edition was a safe business proposition, Falconer (physician at Bath General Hospital) having a wide reputation as a research-minded investigator. Opposite on the left [Fig.79], the two epigrams are a sample of Meyler's own trite society verse from his *Poetical Amusement on the Journey of Life* issued in 1806. This required no second edition, unlike the third example [Fig.80], a best-seller whist manual that Meyler went on profitably reprinting for many years to come. More surprising jobs also came his way, among them *Canine Biography, or... Anecdotes of Dogs...* (2 vols, 1804) and *A Narrative of... the Storming of Buenos Aires by the British Army* (1807).

TABLE OF
THE EVENTS OF HIP CASES,
RECEIVED INTO
THE BATH HOSPITAL,
FROM MAY 1st, 1785, TO APRIL 7th, 1801.

Ages.	Cured.	Much better.	Better.	No better.	Improper.	Irregular.	Dead.	Total.
Under 10		5	8	1	9			23
10 to 20	30	24	32	9	34		2	131
20 to 30	20	48	28	13	34	2	1	146
30 to 40	22	29	18	2	24	3		98
40 to 50	21	30	15	7	16	3		92
50 to 60	8	25	6	1	5	2	2, 1 of S.-Pox.	49
60 and upw.	2	7	4			3	1 of S.-Pox.	17
Total	103	168	111	33	122	13	6	556 in all

Fig.78

EPITAPH ON A STAYMAKER,

Who killed himself by leaping out of a Window into the back Area
of his House.

His bones beneath poor Foret lays,
  A lifeless, clay-cold lump;
Who, though he lived by making *stays*,
  Yet perish'd by a *jump*.

ON ATTENDING A PARTY OF BEAUTIFUL YOUNG LADIES

TO HEAR

THE MUSICAL GLASSES,

AT THE OLD ROOMS, BATH.

" Did ever mortal, mixture of earth's mould,
" Breath such divine, enchanting ravishment?"
                                        MILTON.

CARTWRIGHT! to sounds thy touch gives birth,
That lift my very soul from earth;
And to my raptured mind 'tis given
T' anticipate the joys of Heaven;
Stronger to make the charm appear—
Angels surround me whilst I hear!

Fig.79

ADVICE
TO THE
YOUNG WHIST PLAYER.
CONTAINING MOST OF THE
Maxims of the Old School,
WITH
THE AUTHOR'S OBSERVATIONS,
ON THOSE
HE THINKS ERRONEOUS:
WITH
SEVERAL NEW ONES,
EXEMPLIFIED
BY APPOSITE CASES;

AND A METHOD OF ACQUIRING A KNOWLEDGE OF THE
PRINCIPLES ON WHICH THEY ARE GROUNDED,

POINTED OUT TO THE
INEXPERIENCED WHIST PLAYER.

THE THIRD EDITION WITH ADDITIONS.

BY THOMAS MATTHEWS, ESQ.

BATH, PRINTED BY W. MEYLER:

AND SOLD BY

G. ROBINSON ; LONGMAN, HURST, REES, AND ORME,
PATERNOSTER-ROW ; AND J. HARDING,
ST. JAMES-STREET, LONDON.

1808.

Fig.80

Bowdler publications and *The Family Shakespeare*

Notorious to later generations as prudish expurgators of literary classics, the Bath Bowdlers enjoyed an altogether different reputation during their lifetime. They were a devout, bookish family – five of them becoming published authors. The mother, Elizabeth Stuart Bowdler, had set the writing example with her contributions to the *Christian Magazine*, though her principal work, *Practical Observations on the Revelation of St John*, appeared only in 1800, printed by Cruttwell after her death. By then Cruttwell had already gained richly from the posthumous publication of *Poems and Essays* by her eldest daughter Jane. This pious work of Christian consolation, penned by a hopeless invalid, had immediate appeal. First issued in 1786 in two Crown octavo volumes, the profits going to the Bath General Hospital, it was widely admired, winning over Queen Charlotte among many others. It went through six editions (or reprints) in three years and by 1815 had reached its fifteenth edition (including a tenth edition in Royal quarto) and was still performing strongly under the watchful eye of its compiler, Jane Bowdler's sister Harriet (i.e. Henrietta Maria). She herself was doing even better meanwhile with her own book, *Sermons on the Doctrines and Duties of Christianity* (1801), which Cruttwell found himself reprinting year after year in two different formats, an octavo priced at 5s. and a duodecimo at 4s., as well as issuing the 'Sermon on the Sacrament' as an excerpted four-penny pamphlet. By 1815 the complete *Sermons* was in its 30th edition.

If the *Sermons* brought Harriet Bowdler fame, the anonymously published *Family Shakespeare* – by deliberate design – did not. The concept of a set of Shakespeare plays shorn of 'every thing unfit to be read aloud' (as the publicity claimed) had its roots in the family gatherings of her childhood when her father would silently amend the Shakespearian text as he read aloud. And though the name of the blue-pencilling editor was never divulged, all the evidence points to Harriet Bowdler in spite of some

vi   PREFACE.

fefs, that his Plays contain much that is vulgar, and much that is indelicate; and that, in compliance with the tafte of the age in which he lived, he inferted fome things which ought to be wholly omitted, and others which might be rendered unexceptionable by a very little alteration. It is juftly obferved, by the author* of that elegant effay, in which SHAKESPEARE is vindicated from the illiberal attacks of VOLTAIRE, that " there are deli-
" cacies of decorum in one age, unknown to another
" age; but whatever is immoral, is equally blame-
" able in all ages; and every approach to obfcenity
" is an offence for which wit cannot atone, nor the
" barbarity or the corruption of the times excufe."
On this principle I have omitted many fpeeches in which SHAKESPEARE has been tempted " to pur-
" chafe laughter at the price of decency," in fcenes, for which all the wit of FALSTAFF can furnifh no apology; but I truft that nothing is omitted which the

_____
* Mrs. MONTAGU.

PREFACE.   vii

reader *ought* to regret. For thofe who objeƈt to fuch alterations, there are many editions of SHAKESPEARE, " with all his imperfeƈtions on his head;" but it is hoped that the prefent publication will be approved by thofe who wifh to make the young reader acquainted with the various beauties of this writer, unmixed with any thing that can raife a blufh on the cheek of modefty.

Twenty of the moft unexceptionable of SHAKE-SPEARE's Plays are here feleƈted, in which *not a fingle line is added*, but from which I have endeavoured to remove every thing that could give juft offence to the religious and virtuous mind. My objeƈt is to offer thefe Plays to the public in fuch a ftate, that they may be read with pleafure in all companies, and placed without danger in the hands of every perfon who is capable of underftanding them. Many vulgar, and all indecent expreffions are omitted; an uninterefting or abfurd fcene is fometimes curtailed; and I have occafionally fubftituted a word

b 2

Fig.81

pretence it was her brother Thomas's work – a pretence necessary to safeguard her reputation in an age of increasing propriety, sensibility, and evangelical censure. A fifty-seven-year-old spinster could hardly admit to having understood, or even noticed, all the profanities, bawdy, and other indelicacies so carefully excluded from the text. Furthermore, she omitted some of the more problematic plays altogether. The four-volume set that Cruttwell turned out in 1807 [Figs.81-82 opposite and below] contained only twenty plays.

Distributed in London by the bookseller Hatchard, it had a subdued reception. The term 'bowdlerise' was not yet coined, nor indeed was it current until well after 1818 when Thomas Bowdler, in his own name, brought out a fully re-edited and re-bowdlerised Shakespeare collection of thirty-six plays. This again attracted little notice, until in 1821 a loud critical dispute over its merits finally propelled *The Family Shakespeare* into the list of nineteenth-century best-sellers – only Cruttwell was not the printer. He did print other titles for the Bowdlers, however, and notably the literary remains of the remarkable linguist Elizabeth Smith after her early death. First came *Fragments in Prose and Verse* in 1808, accompanied by Harriet Bowdler's affectionate tribute, and then in 1809 Smith's translation from the German of the *Memoirs of Frederick and Margaret Klopstock*. Cruttwell later issued the two together in a single set and also printed her translation of the biblical *Book of Job*. Finally in 1815 he printed a couple of items for Thomas Bowdler who lived only intermittently at Bath – a biography of his lifelong friend W.A.Villettes, and a pamphlet warning Britons not to emigrate to France but to consider Malta instead. None of the publications of another brother, the high-church John Bowdler, came his way – though when the latter's abridged moralising tract *Reform or Ruin* was offered gratis to country printers in 1797 Samuel Hazard took advantage and made a three-penny booklet of it. On the other hand Cruttwell did in 1804 print the second edition of Charles Daubeny's *A Guide to the Church*, an influential work that John Bowdler admired, defended and thought of abridging.

---

116   MIDSUMMER-NIGHT'S DREAM.   *Act V.*

The. Let us liften to the moon.
Moon. " This lantern doth the horned moon prefent :"
Dem. He fhould have worn the horns on his head.
The. He is no crefcent, and his horns are invifible within the circumference.
Moon. " This lantern doth the horned moon prefent ; " Myfelf the man i' th' moon do feem to be."
The. This is the greateft error of all the reft : the man fhould be put into the lantern. How is it elfe the man i' the moon ?
Hip. I am aweary of this moon. Would, he would change!
The. It appears, by his fmall light of difcretion, that he is in the wane: but yet, in courtefy, in all reafon, we muft ftay the time.
Lys. Proceed, moon.
Moon. All that I have to fay, is, to tell you, that the lantern is the moon; I, the man in the moon; this thorn-bufh, my thorn-bufh; and this dog, my dog.
Dem. Why, all thefe fhould be in the lantern; for they are in the moon. But, filence; here comes Thifbe.

Enter THISBE.

This. " This is old Ninny's tomb. Where is my love?"
Lion. " Oh—."   [*The Lion roars. Thifbe runs off.*
Dem. Well roar'd, lion.
The. Well run, Thifbe.
Hip. Well fhone, moon.—Truly, the moon fhines with a good grace.
The. Well mous'd, lion.
    [*The Lion tears Thifbe's mantle, and exit.*
Dem. And fo comes Pyramus.
Lys. And fo the lion vanifhes.

Enter PYRAMUS.

Pyr. " Sweet moon, I thank thee for thy funny beams; " I thank thee, moon, for fhining now fo bright : " For by thy gracious, golden, glittering ftreams, " I truft to tafte of trueft Thifby's fight.

Scene I. MIDSUMMER-NIGHT'S DREAM.   11;

        " But ftay ;—O fpite!
        " But mark ;—Poor knight,
    " What dreadful dole is here ?
        " Eyes do you fee ?
        " How can it be?
    " O dainty duck ! O dear!
        " Thy mantle good,
        " What, ftain'd with blood ?
    " Approach, ye furies fell!
        " O fates! come, come ;
        " Cut thread and thrum ;
    " Quail, crufh, conclude, and quell!"

The. This paffion, and the death of a dear friend, would go near to make a man look fad.
Hip. Befhrew my heart, but I pity the man.
Pyr. " O, wherefore, nature, didft thou lions frame? " Since lion vile hath here deflour'd my dear : " Which is—no, no—which was the faireft dame, " That liv'd, that lov'd, that lik'd, that look'd, with cheer.
        " Come, tears, confound ;
        " Out, fword, and wound
    " The pap of Pyramus :
        " Ay, that left pap,
        " Where heart doth hop:—
    " Thus die I, thus, thus, thus.
        " Now am I dead,
        " Now am I fled ;
    " My foul is in the fky;
        " Tongue, lofe thy light !
        " Moon, take thy flight!
    " Now die, die, die, die, die.   [*Dies.*
                        [*Exit Moonfhine.*
Dem. No die, but an ace, for him; for he is but one.
Lys. Lefs than an ace, man; for he is dead; he is nothing.
The. With the help of a furgeon, he might yet recover, and prove an afs.
Hip. How chance moonfhine is gone, before Thifbe comes back and finds her lover?

Fig.82

Wood & Cunningham

In March 1808 Cruttwell advertised for a new apprentice, presumably because one of his current apprentices, George Wood, had come to the end of his seven-year term. After a very brief stint of self-employment Wood teamed up with G[eorge?] Cunningham at 18 Northgate Street, not far from Mary Gye's, where they grandly named themselves the City Printing Office. Since this was a description recently used by William Meyler, it may well be that Cunningham had been working until then for Meyler's establishment. Whatever its origin they clung on to the title as they twice removed over the next two years, first to Stall Street and then in 1811 to permanent quarters at 9 Union Street. Here they also sold all kinds of plain and fancy stationery and a selection of new books.

Their printing career began with a flourish. As early as June 1809 they were printing an intended monthly miscellany, the *Bath and West of England Magazine*, and in November a brand-new local guidebook, *The Improved Bath Guide or Picture of Bath and its Environs* from which the frontispiece illustration above is taken. The miscellany, promoted as 'an agreeable literary manual', almost certainly soon foundered, as was the way with Bath magazines, but the *Improved Bath Guide* did well and progressed into future editions together with a parallel Cheltenham guide.

The first few years, 1809-11, brought in a characteristically varied mix of book commissions. In 1809 they printed part of a legal textbook on the law of *Nisi prius* for a metropolitan firm, sending down the whole print run to London except for 'a few copies... left with the printers for sale in the country'. Two publications of 1810 were done for female authors – the first, by the pseudonymous Lady Letitia Liberal, a defence of the Lancasterian school system to coincide with the opening of the first monitorial school at Bath; the second an apparently true, victim's tale of social ostracism at Bath, written by a Mrs Sydenham Wylde under the novelettish title *Who's to Blame?* The following year the Wood & Cunningham imprint appeared on a miscellaneous volume of fugitive verse; an introduction to the arts and sciences by a Wiltshire schoolmaster; and the chemical analysis of the Bath waters illustrated opposite [Fig.83], its title-page noticeably parading the recently arrived C.H.Wilkinson's credentials. Already proprietor of the Kingston Baths, Wilkinson would go on to mastermind the introduction of gas lighting to the city.

In February 1812 Wood & Cunningham finished printing a medical work, *Observations on the Contracted Intestinum Rectum and the Mode of Treatment,* an octavo with a few engraved plates, by the surgeon of Bath City Infirmary, William White. Previous books by the same author had been printed by the old firms of Hazard, Hazard & Binns, and Cruttwell, but perhaps the assignment went to Wood & Cunningham this time on cheapness or because they had spare printing capacity. Three slim pamphlets of around the same date, contributions to a theatrical squabble, would certainly not have occupied their press for long – *The Rosciad: a Herio-Serio-Comical Poem in two* [separate] *Cantos* by KLMNOPQ, and *The Trial of KLMNOPQ... intended as a XYZ to the Subject* amounted to only 40 pages of print. A rather more demanding job of 1812, William Green's *Plans of Economy, or The Road to Ease and Independence both in Town and Country*, was still only a duodecimo of 126 pages. Nothing they had accomplished so far hinted at greater ambitions or suggested they would have acquired a third partner and launched a newspaper before the end of the year.

ANALYTICAL RESEARCHES

INTO THE PROPERTIES OF THE

Bath Waters,

With a View of evincing a Similarity in the Chemical and Medical Properties of the various Springs which supply the Kingston Pump-Room and Baths, the King's and Queen's Baths, Great Pump-Room, and Hot Baths;

BEING

THE FIRST COMPARATIVE ANALYSIS MADE OF ALL THE HOT SPRINGS:

And from which is deduced that they are Ramifications from one grand unknown Source.

To which are subjoined,

OBSERVATIONS

ON

AFFECTIONS OF THE SPINE,

HIP-CASES, HERNIÆ, CLUB-FEET, &c.

EVINCING THE ADVANTAGES TO BE DERIVED FROM THE PRINCIPLES OF MECHANISM.

BY DR. WILKINSON,

Associate of the Institute of Medicine of Paris, of the Royal College of Surgeons, London, and of the Philosophical Societies of Manchester and Newcastle; Honorary Member of the Agricultural Society of Bath, and of the Physical Societies of Guy's, Bartholomew's, the Lyceum Medicum Londinense, and of the London Philosophical and Mathematical Societies.

BATH: PRINTED BY WOOD AND CUNNINGHAM,

City Printing-Office, Union-Street;

AND SOLD BY ALL OTHER BOOKSELLERS IN BATH,

AND B. CROSBY AND CO. LONDON.

1811.—*Price 4s.*

Fig.83

Wood & Co. and the *Bath and Cheltenham Gazette*

Under the new partnership of Wood, Cunningham and Henry Smith, the first issue of the *Bath and Cheltenham Gazette* appeared on 7 October 1812, the date of the parliamentary elections. As a rule elections caused little stir at Bath, since voting for the city's two M.P.s was restricted to the thirty members of the Corporation and took place in private. This time, however, there was some excitement as John Allen, a well-to-do property owner, mounted a legal challenge to the Corporation by offering himself and a colleague as candidates and holding a mock freemen's election. The following day, when Allen tried to address a crowded meeting in the Marketplace, the authorities intervened, and in the ensuing fracas the Guildhall windows were stoned, six 'rioters' were arrested, and Allen had to be rescued by supporters. All this was highly newsworthy and provoked a flurry of handbills and partisan press reports. A fuller but anonymous defence of Allen's conduct soon appeared – *An Impartial Statement of Facts arising out of... the Mock Election at Bath*, printed by the sympathetic John Browne. Like Browne's earlier publication *Le Papillon* it waxed indignant about the craven deference of Bath's press [Fig.85, opposite], yet here at least Wood & Co. could be absolved, for they too offered a platform for radical voices. They prominently featured, for example, a Bath freeman's letter, forwarded by Allen, in the fourth issue of the *Gazette* on 28 October [Fig.84 below]. More than that, they used the newspaper office to collect signatures to a petition demanding a wider franchise, fair representation, and annual parliaments, and in 1813 printed a radical pamphlet, *A View of Bath, Historical, Political and Chronological*, with a frontispiece portrait of Allen and a title-page vignette of his now notorious Marketplace meeting [Fig.86 opposite].

Otherwise, in looks and content, the *Gazette* was orthodox enough, and notwithstanding opposition from the *Cheltenham Chronicle*, it soon consolidated its position at fast-growing Cheltenham and established a network of distributors in the area – a task familiar to George Wood through his previous experience as a commercial traveller for Cruttwell's *Bath Chronicle*. Though the printing was all done at Bath, the coach service to Cheltenham was now quick and reliable, and a formal link with another spa probably made more business sense than one, say, with maritime, industrial Bristol. By 1814 the future of the *Gazette* seemed secure. That October, Wood & Co. sold off the bookshop and reading room at their Union Street premises to H.B.Evans in order to pay full attention to the *Gazette* and their general printing.

Fig.84

BATH ELECTION.

———

To the Freemen, Citizens, and Inhabitants of Bath, as well as to the Public in general, this plain Statement of Facts *is humbly addressed.*

———

A Gross misrepresentation of the late occurrences in this City, as announced in the Bath Herald, of last Evening, has determined an eye-witness and Citizen to controvert them, and to remove that odium so industriously endeavoured to be attached to the character of Mr. JOHN ALLEN, that worthy Patriot and Independent Man; who has so nobly come forward the Champion of the Freemen of this City. Well-knowing the shameful Vassalage to which the Venal Newspapers of this City are reduced, and that it would be useless to attempt to get it inserted in their Columns, I shall therefore endeavour to have it published in

Fig.85

Fig.86

62

at Talavera. Last year, in our advance to Oporto and the north, Lord Wellington incorporated a Portuguese regiment with each brigade; this year we have a Portuguese brigade to each British division; which latter arrangement is more satisfactory to the officers of the army, as it keeps the troops of the two nations more distinct in common detail, and at the same time admits of a small saving, as they have rations of meat only three times in each week. The proportion, therefore, of British to Portuguese remains the same; but we shall act more in distinct masses.

August 29.—The light division of the army, which was stationed near Almeida, having been attacked by a very commanding French force, were obliged to retire, on the 24th, across the bridge of Almeida, with the loss of about 300 men. I was under the painful necessity of attending to the grave the remains of my poor friend Col. Hull, of the 43d regiment, on the evening of his death. He was shot through the heart, by a musket-ball, early in the action.— The French now being on the banks of the Coa, it became evident that we could no longer remain in our advanced position. On the morning of the 25th, Gen. Crawford and the light division retired to Carvalhal: and about two

63

o'clock A. M, on the 26th, he again retired to Fruxedas; and at the same time we retired from Pinhel to Eerejo, where we hutted for the night. The consternation of the inhabitants of Pinhel, when they knew that we were about to abandon them, cannot well be conceived: the whole population of the town took to flight. Many respectable families were seen, with their servants carrying bundles on their heads, retiring in every direction, having no settled plan but that of avoiding the French. Most of the families of note, amongst others that of my landlord, had hastened their departure after the action of the 24th, as the consequences were inevitable. I have since heard, that the town is completely abandoned.

August 29.—At three o'clock, A. M. we march through Celerico to Linhares. Before you ascend the hill upon which Celerico is situated, you have to cross the Mondego.— The town has its Moorish castle, situated on the most elevated part of the hill, and commanding the course of the Mondego for many miles up the stream. Linhares is about eight miles from Celerico, but it is out of the road, and upon the summit of a lofty hill, immediately under the Sierra d'Estrella, of which it may be said to form

Fig.87

Others join the fray

By the end of 1812 Bath enjoyed the services of around ten letterpress printers, several engraving printers, and maybe a dozen booksellers and stationers (with and without libraries), not to speak of print dealers, music shops selling and lending sheet music and songbooks, and street hawkers peddling broadsheets, ballads and cheap pamphlets. At Combe Down there was even a paper mill, the De Montalt Mill, producing fine Bath vellum writing stock as well as drawing papers that met the standards of Turner, Constable, Cotman, and other artists. Under way from 1805, this ambitious venture was run by a partnership of John Bally (a Milsom Street bookseller and stationer), William Ellen (a porcelain merchant, also of Milsom Street), and George Steart (the former Bath printer) who had shown an earlier interest in quality papers and who probably oversaw the actual manufacture.

The arrival of the *Bath & Cheltenham Gazette* in 1812 gave readers an unprecedented four different local newspapers to choose from. The *Bath Journal* was continued from late September 1808 by Richard Keene, whose stepmother, Ann Keene, had ceased printing it once the Court of Chancery had ruled the paper was a trust concern. She removed to Union Street instead and opened a bookshop and printing office with her former printer, Thomas Wood, but was bankrupt by February 1811, forcing Wood to look elsewhere. Like the *Journal* and *Gazette*, Meyler's *Bath Herald* and Cruttwell's *Bath Chronicle* filled their densely packed four pages with ever more victorious details of the campaigns against Napoleon, a growing quantity of local news, and an unremitting flow of profitable advertisements. The *Herald* was now published by 'Meyler & Son' from Abbey Churchyard – the 26-year-old Thomas Salway Meyler having been made a partner in summer 1808 at the time Meyler's bookshop and circulating library moved from Orange Grove to 'much superior accommodation' next to the Pump Room. The *Chronicle* remained in the safe hands of R.S.Cruttwell who continued furthering his business career. Already a Bath Commissioner (a role that must have opened up investment opportunities), he had recently opened a Stamp (Duty) Office after being awarded a government contract, and in 1810 he purchased a haulage firm running fast and slow wagons on the busy Bristol-Bath-London route – a move that no doubt saved him much future outlay on print and paper transport.

Among the other printers, John Binns – Hazard's successor at the Cheap Street bookshop and library – may have relied mainly on jobbing by 1810, whereas Mary Gye (later Gye & Son) and John Browne still welcomed larger commissions, and the Gye press indeed renewed its stock of type in 1808 expressly to equip it for 'book work' on top of commercial printing. These three were joined in autumn 1810 by a further contender, Benjamin Higman, now setting up on his own account in Upper Borough Walls, probably after a spell working for Meyler. Higman made a point of his expertise in copperplate printing, but what survives of his early work is mostly letterpress, including the example on the left [Fig.87] from Henry Mackinnon, *Journal of the Campaign in Portugal and Spain*, printed in 1812 for the Milsom Street bookseller, Charles Duffield. He successfully established his niche in the printing market, and in 1815 transferred operations to roomier, more visible premises on New Bond Street. Obscurer figures also survived somehow. John Hume, who opened a modest printing office in Westgate Street in 1804, was still in competition five years later after removing to Union Passage and buying extra new type from London. Thomas Whitford, described in 1809 as a ballad printer, worked for many years in the poorer neighbourhood of Avon Street. He may well have been the printer John Salmon's associate from the 1770s. Not a scrap of print from either man is known, the sad fate of most 'printed ephemera'.

Higman's rolling press faced competition from the specialist engraver-printers. The father of engraving at Bath, William Hibbert, died aged 84 or so in 1808, but John and Charles Hibbert continued independently, the former in Chapel Row, the latter further out of town in Margaret's Place. The Hibberts' old rival, William Gingell, was still going strong in Northumberland Place after more than twenty-five years, and several other engravers and copperplate printers had ventured onto the scene. The presence of Abraham Farthing and Richard Hancock around 1800 and of Dowle around 1812 is known solely from the Bath directories, but John Lockyer Huntley at 8 Queen Street by 1809, and a decade later at 2 Pulteney Bridge, also advertised his services in the press – engraved banknotes, headed shop bills, maps and charts, and tradesmen's and visiting cards priced expensively at 2s.4d. to 4s.9d. per hundred. In general the intaglio engravers probably used mixed techniques (line-engraving, drypoint, etching) as William Hibbert, originally much influenced by the famous Thomas Worlidge, had always done. Whether any of them also produced relief woodcuts and wood-engravings is unclear, but if not, who did?

Experiment with lithography

What earned Bath a modest place in the annals of lithography was partly an accident of geology, i.e. the existence of easily quarried White Lias stone in the locality. Lithographs differed from traditional print media in being reproduced from a flat, smooth surface that had to be equally absorbent to grease and water. These conditions were fulfilled in the close-grained White Lias, as Henry Bankes explained in the first slim treatise on the subject, *Lithography, or The Art of making Drawings on Stone for… being multiplied by Printing*, issued by Wood & Co. in 1813 [Fig.88 below]. Yet there was another, more compelling reason for Bath involvement – the enthusiasm of its leading artist, Thomas Barker, who had been fascinated by lithography's potential ever since Senefelder's invention was introduced to Britain in 1800. With Barker's encouragement, the current holder of the British patent, D.J.Redmond, moved from London to Bath probably early in 1813, set up a workshop, and began to experiment with Barker's drawings of country folk – the subject of the first trial publication. The subscription terms for *Forty Lithographic Impressions… of Rustic Figures* appeared in May 1813 and informed potential customers that printing in this novel way, directly from the artist's drawing on the stone, would preserve 'all the

7

great abundance in the immediate neighbourhood of Bath, being the stratum lying under the blue-lias, or layer, which is used for burning into lime, paving the streets, and coarse walling. The white-lias is not so favorable for any of these purposes, and is therefore thought of very little value, except where the other cannot be got.

For the purpose of Lithography, however, no other stone is so eligible. Its application to this art, therefore, will give it a new value, and claim for it a greater share of attention. It takes a very good polish, is compact, fine grained, and absorbent of water. It may be procured of any superficial dimensions required.

Previous to my entering more minutely into the practice of the art, I shall notice its more prominent and obvious capacity, viz. that of multiplying the drawing from

Fig.88

Fig.89

spirit and effect of the Originals'. The edition would cost subscribers three guineas and be ready in July. In fact it eventually came out in December with only 117 of the 200 copies subscribed for, and expectations for the next Barker title must accordingly have been muted. So it was that the print-run of *Thirty-two Lithographic Impressions... of Landscape Scenery* was limited to only fifty copies, and the complete volume, published in spring 1814, cost an almost prohibitive six guineas. The actual lithographs were larger than those in the volume of *Rustic Figures* [Fig.89 above is an example from *Landscape Scenery*], but otherwise the presentation was similar. Barker's images were impressed onto sheets of thin china paper which were then individually pasted onto sturdier paper to appear on the recto of each opening like a collection of separate prints bound up. *Landscape Scenery* had a pictorial title-page also printed by Redmond, with Wood & Co. contributing just a small amount of letterpress to each volume.

Nevertheless the economics of the operation hardly made sense. The artistic and technical achievement met with scant financial reward, and only one more lithographic publication was attempted, *Eight Lithographic Impressions* by different local artists – including one from the engraver John Hibbert trying his hand at a quite different medium. Barker, however, seems to have lost interest in the project, while Redmond, after trying to sustain himself at Bath with jobbing work, returned to London in 1815.

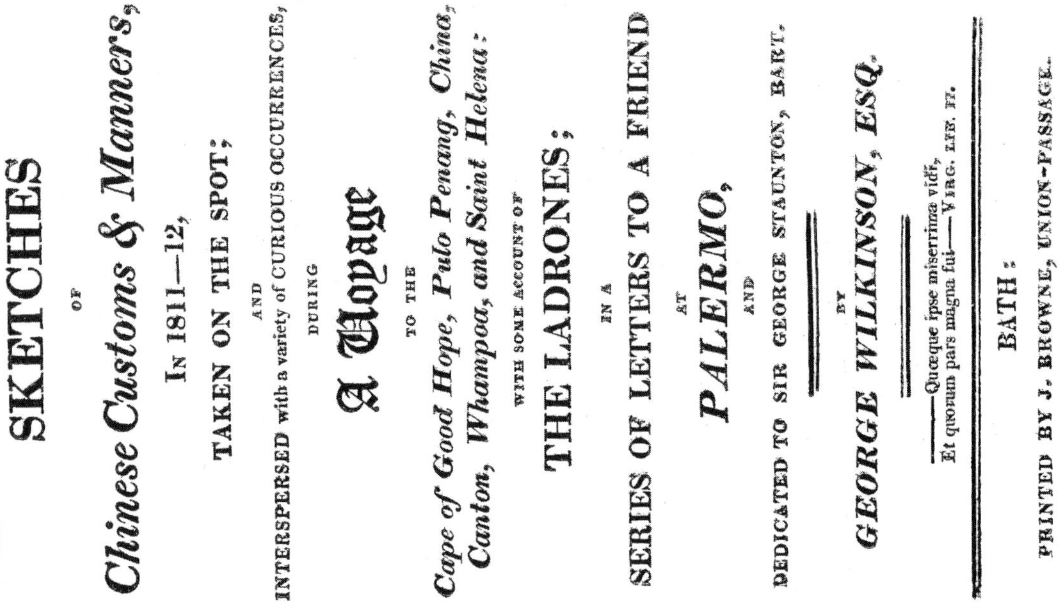

SKETCHES

OF

Chinese Customs & Manners,

IN 1811—12,

TAKEN ON THE SPOT;

AND

INTERSPERSED with a variety of CURIOUS OCCURRENCES,

DURING

A Voyage

TO THE

Cape of Good Hope, Pulo Penang, China, Canton, Whampoa, and Saint Helena:

WITH SOME ACCOUNT OF

THE LADRONES;

IN A

SERIES OF LETTERS TO A FRIEND

AT

PALERMO,

AND

DEDICATED TO SIR GEORGE STAUNTON, BART.

BY

GEORGE WILKINSON, ESQ.

——— Quæque ipse miserrima vidi,
Et quorum pars magna fui.——— VIRG. LIB. II.

BATH:

PRINTED BY J. BROWNE, UNION-PASSAGE.

AND SOLD BY ALL BOOKSELLERS.

1814.

Fig.90

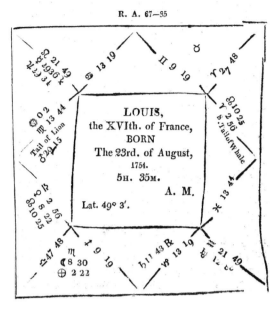

Fig.91

John Browne

For a decade and more John Browne had been known to the Bath reading public as a bookseller, as librarian to the short-lived gentleman's subscription library, as compiler and publisher of two editions of the *New Bath Directory*, and as printer of a magazine, *Le Papillon*, and a dozen or so books, including a few oddities rather typical of lists of Bath imprints at this period. Reproduced above [Fig.91], the slapdash-looking horoscope of the guillotined Louis XVI appeared in a 436-page handbook by the astrologist Thomas White, *The Beauties of Occult Science Investigated, or The Celestial Intelligencer*, printed by Browne about 1810. The title-page opposite [Fig.90] speaks for itself, yet leaves in doubt who financed this 386-page octavo unless the author himself. Perhaps more intriguing is the facing frontispiece portrait ascribed 'WH Bath' – this in a publication dated 1814, six years after the engraver William Hibbert's death. John Browne was working by then in obscurer premises off Cheap Street, having retreated from his former prominent shop on Bridge Street and seemingly given up bookselling. Here in 1815 he printed (for an anonymous author) another rather quirky compilation, *The Oracles of the Ancients Explained wherein a True Answer may be obtained to any Question whatsoever*.... Produced in small folio, it required him to set an extensive series of tables [as in the excerpt below, Fig.92] that offered clues to lines of verse printed later in the book.

THEOPHRASTUS.

	1	1	1		1	1	6		3	3	6		5	5	3
		Mars				Pisces				Taurus				Aries	
93		IV.		*97*		XXXII.		*67*		XXXII.		*65*		LIII.	
	6	5	1		5	4	1		2	2	2		2	2	1
		Cancer				Sol				Taurus				Libra	
71		LI.		*99*		XXXIV.		*67*		III.		*77*		XXVI.	
	4	4	1		5	5	4		6	5	2		5	4	2
		Sagitare				Leo				Sol				Sol	
91		XI.		*73*		IX.		*99*		XXXII.		*99*		XLIII.	
	3	3	3		2	2	3		4	4	2		5	5	6
		Taurus				Sol				Scorpio				Pisces	
67		IV.		*99*		XIV.		*79*		XXIV.		*97*		V.	
	6	5	3		5	4	3		4	4	4		2	2	4
		Venus				Sol				Mercury				Sagitare	

Fig.92

Gye & Son/Henry Gye

The picture below [Fig.93] portrays Gye's shop at 13 Marketplace as it looked in 1819. It reveals what appears to be a glazed roof extension, perhaps built after 1816 (when London-based Frederick, Mary Gye's eldest printer son, won a lottery fortune) and surely housing the printing office despite the weight of the equipment. Hemmed in on the south and behind by the *Christopher* inn, the premises were otherwise fairly cramped for they also contained an extensive wholesale and retail stationery shop. The latter had always been a vital adjunct to the business, and since 1809 had sold among many other products the hot-pressed and vellum papers made at the local De Montalt mill.

In 1813 the 26-year-old Henry Gye joined his mother, Mary, as full partner in the firm, and in 1815 took over entirely. Technically he was one of the more adventurous Bath printers, even printing a few items (e.g. stanzas of verse) on silk. In the two illustrations opposite [Figs.94-95] from Edward Mangin's *Utopia Found* (1813), the title-page words 'UTOPIA FOUND' were originally executed in dramatic red ink and faced an equally dramatic cartoon-like frontispiece, while a 'copperplate' fount was employed in the body of the text to simulate hand-written correspondence.

Fig.93

In 1815 he bought twenty founts of quite new type and probably exchanged a Demy for a larger Double Crown press. It would, however, be a small hand machine he used at the thronged victory fête of 6 July 1814 on Claverton Down, where he publicly ran off broadsheets of patriotic verse – at least some of them printed on silk – bearing the temporary imprint of the 'Wellington Press' [see the ink-smudged excerpt overleaf, Fig.96].

The portrait of the former Bath stone-mason Thomas Parsons [also overleaf, Fig.97] made a handsome frontispiece to the obituary sermon on Parsons preached by William Jay of Argyle Chapel, printed by Gye in 1813 under the title *The Loss of Connexions deplored and improved....* Here Gye has turned to the Bristol engraver and miniaturist, Nathan Branwhite, whose translation of the original painting into print looks far more accomplished than anything the Bath engravers were capable of. Gye had been William Jay's regular printer ever since 1805, producing a whole string of sermons and other works, among them the *Short Discourses to be read in Families* issued in several editions, octavo and duodecimo, 1805-17. Several other notable authors – Edward Mangin, John Trusler, and Joseph Townsend – took him their manuscripts, and with Townsend he accomplished one of his most significant books, *The Character of Moses established for Veracity as an Historian*, a two-volume work of nearly 900 pages and 21 plates. Though Townsend was a clergyman he was a geologist as well, and in the course of reconciling the rocks with *Genesis*, he brought his old friend William Smith back into notice, leading to Smith's great geological map of England and Wales being published at last.

UTOPIA FOUND:

BEING

An Apology

FOR

IRISH ABSENTEES.

Addressed to a Friend in Connaught

BY AN ABSENTEE,

Residing in Bath.

Do not smile at me that I boast her off;
For thou shalt find she will outstrip all praise,
And make it halt behind her.
SHAKSPEARE'S TEMPEST.

Printed by Gye and Son, Market-Place, Bath.

1813.

Fig.94

88

shells, and cabbage roses; to talk, filthily, in corrupt French, and mewl Italian nonsense over a *Piano!* I here cannot resist the opportunity of presenting you with a copy of part of a letter from one of these thorough bred female botanists to another of her own class: it got abroad, I know not how, and excited much laughter amongst these high minded and rational English. The accomplished writer is (I believe) describing to her Correspondent, the Magnolia, and, (as she herself expresses it) in the plainest terms she could find.

" *You must understand, my sweet Prissy, that these are all Polyandria Polygnia, and are placed in the natural order of coadunatæ. In*

Fig.95

ADDRESS
IN COMMEMORATION OF PEACE
BETWEEN
Russia, Austria, Prussia, Sweden, France, and England.

Printed by GYE and SON, *of the Market-Place, Bath,*

At the Wellington Press,

In the Centre of CLAVERTON-DOWN, near BATH,

On WEDNESDAY, JULY 6, 1814;

All the Parishes appear,
Come to hail *the* PARISH here !
PEACE, with PARISH in her train,
Comes to bless old BLADUD's plain.

See the feasts they now prepare,
Hark ! the shouts that rend the air!
See the bill directs the way
To the sports prepar'd to-day:
This day, by British valour wou—
Led by godlike WELLINGTON !

All the laurels we have won—
All the good your ZEAL has done—
See the PRINTERS too appear
On the spot recording here !
Now's the time to tell your SON
The *triumphs* you for him have won—
TAKE it, place it in his hand—
That HE, like YOU, may prove a BLESSING to the LAND!

W. H. P.

Fig.96

Fig.97

Meyler & Son

When in 1808 they relocated their bookshop and library to newly built premises in Abbey Churchyard, William and T.S.Meyler also obtained a 21-year lease of the adjacent vaults under the Pump Room. Early in 1809 they asked the Corporation for a piece of land just east of the King's and Queen's Baths on which to erect a low building especially for the printing office, at that point still in Kingston Buildings. Then serving his second term as a city Bailiff, William Meyler might have expected special dispensation, but the application was turned down on grounds of the site's proximity to the baths. Nevertheless he valued his seat on the Council, where T.S.Meyler joined him in 1816. He was made a magistrate in 1818, and might well have risen to the position of Mayor but for incapacitating ill health in the three years up to his death in 1821. He had always been an organisation man, once a keen member of the Batheaston Vase circle, secretary to bodies such as the Bath Guardian Society and Bath Loyal Association, and an active freemason – several times Master of his lodge and even Provincial Grand Registrar of Somerset. The value of masonic ties to business cannot be measured, but other Bath printers too were initiates in their time, Thomas Boddely, the elder John Keene, Stephen Martin (who helped found the Shakespeare Head lodge), and Richard Cruttwell among them.

Besides the *Bath Herald* – their major printing responsibility – and the biennial editions of *The Original Bath Guide*, the Meylers contributed fairly modestly to the annual tally of Bath books, predominantly sermons and books of verse, and from 1812 sundry items for the Bath Auxiliary Bible Society. Less run-of-the-mill were W.J.Hort's *Miscellaneous English Exercises... Prose and Poetry written in False Spelling, False Grammar, and without Stops...* (a nice test in 1813 for the compositor and corrector), John Beard's *A Diary of Fifteen Years Hunting... from 1796 to 1811* (likewise printed in 1813), and a short but earnest anonymous pamphlet of 1814, *Bath: a Glance at its Public Worship, Style of Dress, Cotillons, Masquerades, &c. &c.* Part of the latter's dismayed censure of revealing Regency fashion is reproduced below.

12

party, whilst some fluttering beaux were uttering their amusing nothings, with many a laugh, which made the hours seem but as minutes. O let not the solemn Service of the Sanctuary be less reverenced and regarded than the prattle of human beings, which, however perfect in its kind, must yield in importance to the law of God. " Shall not I visit for these things ? saith the Lord."

IT is impossible for a person possessing any feeling or reflection to mix in the public crowds, or even attend private parties in Bath, without the most painful sensations upon the present style of dress, or rather *want* of dress. To behold a row of ladies at an evening assembly, fills the mind with the most fearful apprehensions of an approaching complete dissoluteness of man-

13

ners—approaching did I say ? it is upon us, it has taken possession ; the thing itself is gross dissoluteness of mind ; it is rapidly removing all respect and admiration from the sex ; it is a style of appearance some years back only adopted by the courtezans of the metropolis. Do these self-deluded fair ones imagine that they please the other sex by this dreadful indecency, now arrived at its achme of displaying unkerchiefed as much as possible of the person ? They are most unfortunately mistaken. I would wish to speak plainly and flatter no one. I would it were possible to convince them of the total distaste with which men of all ages behold this lamentable style of appearance. I know it to be so : not being an interested person, I have frequently heard their re-

Fig.98

R.S.Cruttwell

Whatever the efforts of other Bath printers, Cruttwell remained top dog. He produced far more books than any of his rivals; his *Bath Chronicle* was probably the most read and regionally influential of the four local newspapers; and he did his share of jobbing work – exemplified [Fig.100 opposite] in a detail from a beautifully executed poster that deployed six different founts in as many lines without any fussiness or loss of elegance. The same clean, classic setting of good type can be appreciated below [Fig.99] in a page from Thomas Broadhurst's *Funeral Orations in Praise of Military Men* also printed in 1811. Like the Dress Ball poster, this displays the standard letter 's' throughout, but it is a curiosity of Cruttwell's output at this period that the old-fashioned 'long s' still turned up from time to time, even as late as 1815 in the case of *Collections relative to the Systematic Relief of the Poor*, compiled by J.S.Duncan and printed for the London publisher Murray [shown in an extract opposite, Fig.101]. Might one infer from this the presence in the printing shop of an older compositor unwilling to change his ways?

Cruttwell's staff were accustomed nonetheless to occasional refreshing of the stock of type. This would next occur in 1817 expressly for the visit to Bath of Queen Charlotte, a rare royal event that prompted Cruttwell to have new type specially cast for the *Chronicle*. The result, as one contemporary judged it, was 'a *chef d'oeuvre* in newspaper printing'. Production was still by the traditional, laborious, hand press method that set practical limits to print-runs, but Cruttwell had already spied the writing on the wall. A long admiring paragraph in the *Chronicle* of 15 December 1814 described how the daily London *Times* was now produced on a cylinder steam press capable of running off over 1100 wonderfully clear impressions per hour, with minimal human effort and at five times the rate of a conventional press. It was a machine that Cruttwell could only dream of at present.

FUNERAL ORATION

OF

PLATO.ᵃ

THE obsequies, due to these men, have now been strictly performed; and, having received them,ᵇ they go the way

---

ᵃ The introductory dialogue to this Oration, between Socrates and Menexenus, the translator has judged proper to omit; as being, from its ironical and humourous strain, unsuitable to the dignity and gravity of the subsequent sentiments. Socrates is there introduced by Plato, as pronouncing, from memory, the harangue which he had heard Aspasia deliver, partly from premeditation, and partly extempore, in honour of the heroes who had

Fig.99

Dress Ball.

1811---1812.

SUBSCRIPTION for 24 BALLS,

EVERY MONDAY DURING THE SEASON,

ON THE FOLLOWING TERMS:

A Subscription of FOURTEEN SHILLINGS will entitle the Subscriber to Admission each Ball Night.

A Subscription of TWENTY-SIX SHIL-

Fig.100

with referring for farther information to page 44 of his useful book.

Edinburgh abounds in charitable establishments, some of which it may be interesting to enumerate, with a view of considering how large a sum they supply toward the aid of the poor.

Heriot's Hospital, the funds of which are applied to the education, and placing out in various ways, of boys, of whom above 100 are in the house.

Watson's Hospital, for the same purposes.

Merchants' Maiden Hospital, for girls.

Trades' Maiden Hospital, on a similar plan to the preceding.

Orphan Hospital maintains above 150; empowered to hold real property of 1000l. per ann.; supported by charitable contributions.

Gillespie's Hospital, for old men and women, and for the education of 100 boys.

Trinity Hospital, for the reception of poor aged burgesses, their widows and daughters, maintains about fifty.

Fig.101

Bath imprints, 1814-1815

Sorted by subject, a list of books and pamphlets printed in Bath around 1815 reveals something of the interests and preoccupations of the time, though it makes no claim to be a complete record. The majority are Cruttwell imprints. Where they are not, the printer is named in brackets.

Sermons and religious topics
  W.L.Bowles, *Sermons respecting the Faith, the Feelings...*
  J.Calderbank, *Observations... relating to... Religion proposed... to a Catholic Convert* [Gye & Son]
  W.Jay, *The Importance of an Evangelical Ministry* [Gye & Son]
  W.Jay, *A Selection of Hymns... for... Argyle Chapel* [Gye & Son]
  W.Jay, *Sermons*, 4th ed. [Gye & Son]
  F.E.King, *Female Scripture Characters exemplifying Female Virtues*
  T.Roberts, *The Burning and Shining Light* [Meyler & Son]
  A Short Letter on the Nomination of a Rector of Bath [Gye & Son]
  R.Warner, *Charity, or Christian Love... a Sermon*
  R.Warner, *Diligence, its Nature and Advantages: a Sermon*
  R.Warner, *Divine Favour claims Religious Gratitude: a Sermon...*
  R.Warner, *Divine Providence exemplified in... the late War: a Sermon*
  R.Warner, *Preparation for Death the Great Business of Life: a Sermon...*
  W.B.Whitehead, *General Education the Basis for... Happiness: a Sermon*

Economics
  An Address to the Inhabitants of Bath on the Subject of Bread...
  Bath and West of England Society, *Letters and Papers on Agriculture... v.13*
  J.Benett, *An Essay on the Commutation of Tithes...*
  Charge to the Grand Jury of...Wexford...containing...Advice to...Absentee Landowners [Gye & Son]
  W.Clark, *An Enquiry into the Causes that have impeded... Arable Farms...*
  W.Clark, *Thoughts on the Commutation or Abolition of Tithes*
  W.Clark, *Thoughts on the Management and Relief of the Poor...*
  [J.S.Duncan], *Collections relative to Systematic Relief of the Poor at Different Periods...*
  R.Gourlay, *The Right to Church Property secured... Commutation of Tithes vindicated* [Gye & Son?]
  [R.Gourlay], *The Tyranny of the Poor Law exemplified* [Gye & Son]

Society and behaviour
  Anti-Prosopopoeia, or The Ghost of Beau Nash... [Meyler & Son]
  Bath: a Glance at its Public Worship, Style of Dress, Cotillons... 1st-2nd eds. [Meyler & Son]
  Remarks on Modern Female Manners [Meyler & Son]

History and travel
  T.Bowdler, *Observations on Emigration to France...* 1st-2nd eds.
  J.Toulmin, *An Historical View of... the Protestant Dissenters in England...*
  J.Townsend, *A Journey through Spain in the Years 1786 and 1787...* 3rd ed., 2v. [Gye & Son]
  H.Wansey, *A Visit to Paris in June 1814*
  G.Wilkinson, *Sketches of Chinese Customs and Manners in 1811-12...* [Browne]

Biography
  T.Bowdler, *A Short View of the Life... of Lieutenant-General Villettes*
  R.Hoare, *A Journal of the Shrievalty of Richard Hoare, Esquire... 1740-41*

Medicine and Science
  O.W.Bartley, *Observations on the... Saline and Chalybeate Spas at Melksham*
  C.H.Parry, *Cases of Tetanus and Rabies Contagiosa...*
  C.H. Parry, *Elements of Pathology and Therapeutics, v.1*
  J.Townsend, *The Character of Moses established for Veracity as an Historian* [by geology], v.2 [Gye & Son]
  W.White, *Observations on Strictures... with Cases and Engravings*, 2nd ed. [H.Gye]

Language
  W.Robertson, *Robertson's Compendious Hebrew Dictionary*, ed. N.Joseph
  T.Wilkins, *The Rules for the Declension of Latin Nouns and Conjugations of Verbs*

Literature
  C.Ash, *Adbaston: a Poem* [Meyler & Son]
  T.Ashe, *The Flagellator: a Philippic... for the Author of 'The Intercepted Epistle'...* [Higman]
  Ellen: a Ballad founded on a Recent Fact, and other Poems
  [R.Graves], *The Coalition, or The Opera rehears'd; a Comedy in Three Acts* [Fig.102 below]
  H.Lawton, *Poems*
  E.Mangin, *A View of the Pleasures arising from a Love of Books* [Gye & Son]
  E.Mangin, *An Intercepted Epistle from a Person at Bath...* 1st-3rd eds. [Gye & Son]
  [R.Warner], *The Omnium-Gatherum, or Bath... Literary Repository*, nos 1-7

Other topics
  T.Barker, *Thirty-two Lithographic Impressions... of Landscape Scenery* [Redmond; Wood & Co]
  The Oracles of the Ancients explained... [Browne]
  The Original Bath Guide [for 1815] [Meyler & Son]

THE

COALITION;

OR,

THE OPERA REHEARS'D.

A COMEDY,

IN THREE ACTS.

BY THE

EDITOR OF THE SPIRITUAL QUIXOTE.

————Valeat res ludicra!

HOR.

BATH, PRINTED BY R. CRUTTWELL,
AND SOLD BY
C. DILLY, POULTRY; and G. G. J. and J. ROBINSON, PATER-
NOSTER-ROW, LONDON.
M DCCCXIV.

Fig.102

CORRECTED TO JANUARY, 1819.   **13**

Labigne, French teacher, 17, *Beaufort-square*
Le Gris, French teacher, 31, *Stall-street*
Lucille, Madame de, French teacher, 5, *George-street*
Richards, Miss, French teacher, 17, *York-street*
Rook, Miss, French and English teacher, 1, *Burlington-street*
Stocker, Miss, French teacher, 33, *St. James's parade*

PROFESSORS OF DANCING.

Ashley, Mr. 4, *Daniel-street*
* Cobb, Mr. 3, *Abbey-green*
* Comer, Miss, 12, *Milsom-street*
* Cranfeldt, Miss, *Milsom-street*
* Giroux, Misses, 14, *George-street*
Jones, Miss C. *Claremont-place, Pulteney-road*

Hobson, Miss, (conductress of the Quadrilles at the Upper Assembly Rooms) 13, *Rivers-street*
* Saunders, Mr. 16, *Queen-square*
* Thomas, Miss, 13, *Gay-street*
* Webster, Mr. 1, *Grove*
* Wingrove, Miss A. 9, *Union-street*

Those marked thus * have academies.

CIRCULATING LIBRARIES.

Barratt and Son, Messrs. *Bond-street*
Collings, Mr. C. B. *Saville-row*
Duffield, Mr. C. *Milsom-street*
Gibbons, Mr. T. *Argyle-buildings*
Godwin, Mr. H. *Milsom-street*

Griffiths, Mr. J. *Argyle-buildings*
Meyler & Son, Messrs. *Abbey church-yard*
Simms, Mr. S. *North-parade*
Upham, Mr. J. *Walks*

BATH WEEKLY NEWSPAPERS.

Which are circulated in Somersetshire, Wiltshire, Gloucestershire, Hampshire, Dorsetshire, Devonshire, &c. and received by the principal booksellers in all the neighbouring market-towns, by whom, advertisements and articles of intelligence are duly forwarded.

The BATH JOURNAL published on Sunday Evening, by Mr. Keene, 7, *Kingsmead-street.*

The BATH AND CHELTENHAM GAZETTE, published on Tuesday Evening, by Messrs. Wood, Cunningham, and Smith, 9, *Union-street.*

The BATH CHRONICLE, published on Wednesday Evening, by Mr. Cruttwell, *St. James's-street*, near *St. James's Church.*

The BATH HERALD, published on Friday Evening, by Messrs. Meyler and Son, adjoining *the Great Pump-room.*

Small parcels are conveyed by the newsmen belonging to the above establishments, to most of the towns, villages, and gentlemen's seats, at reasonable distances, in the counties of Somerset, Wilts, and Gloucester.

Fig.103

After 1815

An epochal date in national and European history, 1815 is also a convenient point to close this account, even though it marks no moment of significant change in the fortunes of Bath printers. Indeed the accent there was on continuity. Technical advances in iron-frame presses, steam-powered printing, and stereotyping had yet to impact on traditional methods. For a while the cast of local printers remained much the same. The four weekly newspapers came out on their customary different days in their usual fashion – as the page from Henry Gye's *Bath Directory* of 1819 witnesses [Fig.103 enlarged]. Jobbing work of all kinds kept the presses busy – engraved visiting cards, circulars, billheads, labels, prospectuses, business reports, large placards and other public notices – together with a good sprinkling of catalogues, brochures, pamphlets and miscellaneous books. Bath was still growing (though at a slower rate than in the phenomenal later eighteenth century) with little sign of the social decline to come and plenty of evidence still of entrepreneurial and intellectual vigour.

Changes in its printing community became more obvious from around 1820, by which date John and James Keene had already replaced Richard Keene at the *Bath Journal*. There were several deaths and other departures. Meyler & Son – who had optimistically bought new type from Edinburgh in 1819 – suffered a double blow. The long-ailing William Meyler died in 1821 and his 42-year-old son T.S.Meyler in 1823, leaving the latter's widow, Mary Meyler, to run the firm and continue the *Bath Herald* from then on – very successfully as it turned out. When Henry Gye also died young in 1823, the Gye name failed to be perpetuated, though, since his brother Edmund, rather than take over himself, sold the Marketplace shop and printing office as a going concern to Charles Hunt. Two years later George Wood of the *Bath & Cheltenham Gazette* had to adjust to the departure of his two partners Cunningham and Smith, the former going on to found an independent printing office in New King Street. Nor was the august *Bath Chronicle* immune to change as R.S. Cruttwell handed over the management of the business to Frederick Collier Bakewell in autumn 1828 while remaining overall proprietor.

Pigot & Co.'s *National Commercial Directory* of 1830 listed twelve letterpress printers at Bath. Some of them were familiar names from the past. Ann E.Binns, Samuel Hazard's daughter, was still running the bookshop and circulating library in Cheap Street (with printing on the side) following John Binns's death in 1822/3. John Browne, Benjamin Higman, Mary Meyler and the two Keenes were all active, as was George Wood too despite not featuring in Pigot & Co.'s list. Among the others who did, F.C.Bakewell and Charles Hunt, successors respectively to Cruttwell and Gye, were now well established, while several newer names – Samuel Bennett, William Browning, William Clark, and Ebenezer Smith – indicated the continuing strong local demand for print. And in addition to these letterpress businesses the list recorded as many as eight 'Engravers and Copperplate Printers', of whom William Gingell alone had survived from earlier days.

Index of printers, publishers and engravers working at Bath

Acknowledgment

Over the years this project has entailed much finding, much fetching, and much re-shelving of the many Georgian imprints requested by the author. Warm thanks are due to all the library staff involved, at Bath City Library and elsewhere, for so cheerfully supplying a sometimes awkward customer.

Sources of information

Many copies of the books, pamphlets and ephemera printed at Bath in the period can still be found in Bath Central Library and other collections, and these have formed the basis for this study. Almost equally important have been files of contemporary Bath newspapers, not only for their own printing history but also for much essential information about local publications, printers, booksellers, etc. contained in their pages. Bath directories, parish registers, property deeds, Bath Council minutes and Chamberlain's accounts, all yielded further details. Among other reference sources and secondary works consulted, the most useful and relevant are listed below. Of these Tyler and Kite offer summary information on Bath printers and booksellers of the period.

Anstey, Christopher, *An Election Ball...* Ed. G. Turner (Bristol, 1997).

British Library, *General Catalogue of Printed Books.*

Cranfield, G.A., *The Development of the Provincial Newspaper, 1700-1760* (Oxford, 1962).

Cranfield, G.A., *The Press and Society: from Caxton to Northcliffe* (London, 1978).

Feather, John, *The Provincial Book Trade in Eighteenth-century England* (Cambridge, 1985).

Gaskell, Philip, *A New Introduction to Bibliography* (Oxford, 1962).

Green, Emanuel, *Bibliotheca Somersetensis.* 3v. (Taunton, 1902), v.1 Bath Books.

Henrey, Blanche, *British Botanical and Horticultural Literature before 1800.* 3v. (London, 1975).

Johnson, J., *Typographia, or The Printers' Instructor.* 2v. (London, 1824).

Kite, V.J., 'Libraries in Bath, 1618-1964' (unpublished thesis, 1964) [Bath Central Library].

Maxted, Ian, *The British Book Trades,1710-1777* (Exeter, 1983).

Oxford Dictionary of National Biography.

Perrin, Noel, *Dr Bowdler's Legacy: A History of Expurgated Books...* (London, 1970).

Plant, Marjorie, *The English Book Trade.* 3rd ed. (London, 1974).

Plomer, H.R., *Dictionary of Printers and Booksellers, 1726-1775* (London, 1932).

Raven, James, *The Business of Books: Booksellers and the English Book Trade, 1450-1850* (New Haven and London, 2007).

Reed, T.B., *A History of the Old English Letter Foundries...* Ed. A.F.Johnson (London, 1952).

Rivers, Isabel, ed., *Books and their Readers in Eighteenth-century England* (Leicester, 1982).

Rivers, Isabel, ed., *Books and their Readers in Eighteenth-century England: New Essays* (Leicester, 2001).

Stott, Anne, *Hannah More: the First Victorian* (London, 2003).

Thomas, P.D.G., 'The beginning of parliamentary reporting in newspapers, 1768-1774', *English Hist. Review* v.74, 1959, 623-36.

Thomas, P.D.G., 'John Wilkes and the freedom of the press', *Bull. Inst. Hist. Res.* v.33, 1960, 86-98.

Tracy, Clarence, *A Portrait of Richard Graves* (Cambridge, 1987).

Tyler, Jennifer, 'Dictionary of Printers, Booksellers and Printers at Work in Bath... 1664-1830' (unpublished thesis, 1972) [Bath Central Library].

Wiles, R.M., *Freshest Advices: Early Provincial Newspapers in England* (Columbus, Ohio, 1965).

Individual printers

CAMPBELL   Steve Poole, 'Radicalism, loyalism and the "reign of terror" at Bath, 1792-1804', *Bath History* v.3, 1990, 125-7.

CRUTTWELL   Cruttwell, H.A., *The History of the Cruttwell Family of Wokingham... and Bath* (Camberley, 1933).

GYE   De Ferrars, D'Arcy, 'Some MS. References to the ... Families of Evill, Stothert, Gye' [Bath Central Library]; Dawson & Goodall Ltd, *200 Years of Printing* (Bath, 1970); Sydenham, S., 'Bath token issues of the 18th century', *Proc.Bath Nat. Hist. & Antiqu. Field Club* v.10, 1905, 217-19.

HAZARD   Stower, G., *The Printer's Grammar...* (London, 1808); Spinney, G.H., 'Cheap Repository Tracts: Hazard and Marshall edition', *The Library: Trans. Bibliographical Soc.*, Dec 1939, 295-340.

MEYLER   [Hunter, Joseph], *Memoir of William Meyler* (Bath? 1822?).

POPE   Fielding, Henry and Sarah, *The Correspondence.* Ed. M.C.Battestin and C.T.Probyn (Oxford, 1993).

REDMOND   McCallum, Iain, *Thomas Barker of Bath* (Bath, 2003).

SKINNER   Hardy, W.J., 'The book-plates of J.Skinner of Bath', *Bibliographica* v.2, 1896, 422-37.

Also published by RUTON

BATH ADMINISTER'D
Corporation Affairs at the 18th-century Spa

By Trevor Fawcett

Bath, RUTON, 2001
ISBN: 0-9526326-2-4

BATH COMMERCIALIS'D
Shops, Trades and Market at the 18th-century Spa

By Trevor Fawcett

Bath, RUTON, 2002
ISBN: 0-9526326-3-2

Two earlier RUTON titles are out-of-print:

VOICES OF EIGHTEENTH-CENTURY BATH
An Anthology of Contemporary Texts
Illustrating Events, Daily Life and Attitudes
at Britain's Leading Georgian Spa (1995)

BATH ENTERTAIN'D
Amusements, Recreations and Gambling
at the 18th-century Spa (1998)

Orders from booksellers or directly from
RUTON, 25 Northampton Street, Bath BA1 2SW